Cookbook

HOW TO WIN A COWBOY'S HEART

Meals to bring the romance of the West into your home

Kathy Lynn Wills

GIBBS · SMITH

PUBLISHER

SALT LAKE CITY

First edition
98 97 96 95 5 4 3 2 1
Text © 1995 by Kathy Lynn Wills

This is a Peregrine Smith Book, published by
Gibbs Smith, Publisher
P.O. Box 667
Layton, UT 84041

Design by Leesha Jones
Illustrations © 1995 by Linda K. Gage: front cover, pages 7, 27, 49, 85
All other illustrations © 1995 by Linda Bark'karie

Printed and bound in the U.S.A.

Library of Congress Cataloging-in-Publication Data
Wills, Kathy Lynn.
    How to win a cowboy's heart / Kathy Lynn Wills.
    p.   cm.
    Includes index.
    ISBN 0-87905-694-0
    1. Cookery, American—Western style. 2. Entertaining.
    3. Cookery for two. 4. Menus. I. Title.
    TX715.2.W47W55   1995
    641.5978—dc20   95-11520
                                                          CIP

Contents

Acknowledgements

Thank you to my friends who valiantly tasted and tried through scorched stews and soggy crusts to lead me onto better work.

To the gang at La Porte's favorite gathering spot, Woodstock Feed: Gene Michaud and the endless search for cinnamon and raisins, Charlie Gann who always has another idea (and another cup of coffee), Roger Clark for funny stories and faithful encouragement ("It's the altitude, Kath."), and Nancy Feldman who packed boxes, carried groceries, smiled sweetly, and even carted critters to the vet.

I'm sorry to Linda Bark'karie with whom I was often too short on the phone and to, I'm afraid, many other good friends I too often forgot to call. I owe a debt of friendship to both Lindas for their darling illustrations. Thanks also to Mary Rogers, Bill Jacobson (along with Kody and Tober), Rusty Alderson, and Vickie Mullen for making me laugh, and Susan Streaker for encouragement, jokes, and recipes ideas over the fax machine. Oh, these modern times.

How far could I have gotten without Jay and Jill Pollitt, Lou Gile, Scott Beauchemin, Steve Kirklys, and Lisa, Ron, and Shane Rothe? They never doubted I could finish even when I wasn't sure. Faith is a powerful motivator.

Here's to "the girls" for the eggs and to my faithful cowdog, Ezra, who sits close when things aren't going well.

Thanks to my father who in my childhood barbecued and basted, stir-fried and stewed so joyously it must have rubbed off on me—and to Grandma Mary. My somewhat hazy memories of her near legendary kitchen inspired many of the enclosed recipes…and of course a warm hug to my favorite family of eaters, John, Carole, Jessie, and Alexa—it's wonderful being your sister and aunt.

I'm grateful to the authors whose quotes brighten these pages, to the editors and staff of Gibbs Smith Publishing, especially Madge, Dawn, and the Susans, and to my mom, who read these words over and over again…each time as if they were new.

A toast to you, my friends.

Ring the Dinner Bell

"A man can stay with a rough outfit a long time," says lifetime cowboy Roger Clark, *"if there are good horses and good food."*

Though some cowhands lament they were "born a hundred years too late," for most women, our modern liberation along with a host of time-saving appliances, brought welcome relief from seemingly endless household chores. I stir up cakes and create new recipes not because it is traditional women's work (in fact, many of the great western cooks from ranch wagons to fifty-acre homesteads were and are men), but because I enjoy it.

If you are a better horseshoer than pot wrassler, by all means take up hammer and nails. If you, like I am, are better at building biscuits than fences, perhaps you'll find a hungry cowboy, mechanic, accountant, or plumber ready to share your table.

More than a primer on authentic cowboy style, this book is about sharing the comfort of good company over a wonderful meal. In the same way that a buckaroo tackles his job holding firmly to tradition and tools of the past, these simple meals flavored by our history and legends, are tasty forget-me-nots from a young nation's love affair with open air, country, cattle, and freedom.

New York City's culinary chiefs may frown on the idea, but western cooks routinely use canned and dried ingredients. Ours is a cuisine born of distance and availability—mostly the distance between wagon or ranch and grocery store and the few items offered for sale. Though today few of us live a day's ride from the nearest market, the tradition of simple ingredients well blended into wholesome foods lives on.

I've heard it said there are many ways to a cowboy's heart…fast horses, silver-mounted spurs, or fancy tall-top boots. I can't guarantee these recipes will ensure a lasting love or even a passing fancy, but the quickest and perhaps easiest route is still the perennial favorite, a home-cooked meal.

Come and get it!

A Calico's Shopping Guide

"It's not so much knowing how to tie everything you need onto a horse," explains Ken Smith, a talented hitcher, braider, and working cowboy from Montana. "It's learning to do without what you left behind."

Here is a short list of the "fixin's" I try to have on hand so that unexpected visitors are a welcome pleasure rather than an extra trip to town.

My Spice Rack
Bay leaves
Black pepper
Chili powder
Cinnamon
Cilantro flakes
Cloves, ground and whole
Crushed red pepper flakes
Cumin
Garlic, fresh and powdered
Mace
Nutmeg
Paprika
Parsley flakes
Red (cayenne) pepper
Salt
White pepper

In the Pantry
Baking soda
Baking powder
Beef bullion
Brown sugar
Chicken bullion
Cocoa
Coffee
Corn or vegetable oil
Cornmeal
Dried beans
Dried fruits (raisins, prunes apricots, etc.)
Flour
Grits
Honey
Lard
Molasses
Non-stick cooking spray
Oatmeal
Olives
Olive oil
Onions (white, yellow, red, and pearl)
Pasta
Peanuts
Peanut oil
Popcorn
Potatoes (white, red, and sweet)
Dry buttermilk mix
Rice
Sugar
Syrups (corn and flavored for flapjacks)
Tea
Vegetable shortening (both regular and butter flavored)

In Cans and Jars
Applesauce
Beans
Corn
Cream of chicken soup
Cream of mushroom soup
Creamed corn
Chili tomatoes
Crushed tomatoes
Green chiles
Hominy
Jams and jellies
Peaches
Peanut butter
Pears
Tomato paste
Tomato sauce
White potatoes
Whole tomatoes

In the Freezer
Beef for stew
Blueberries
Breakfast sausage
Broccoli
Butter
Peas
Pork steaks
Green beans
Ground beef
Frozen bread dough
Ice cream
Juice concentrates
Milk (leave out on the counter to thaw)
Mixed vegetables
Tortillas
Whole chicken ready for roasting

In the Refrigerator
Apples
Bacon
Butter
Buttermilk
Carrots
Fresh vegetables and fruit
Margarine
Milk
Salad greens
Salsa
Sour cream
Spring onions

Essential Utensils
Though I've learned to make do, there are a few cooking utensils I insist upon:

Cast-iron Dutch oven or other heavy covered pot
Cookie sheets
Colander
Covered roaster
Iron skillet
Large mixing bowl
Large rectangular pan
Large stock pot
Loaf pan
Muffin or cupcake tin
Pie tin
Sifter
Saucepan with lid
Sharp chopping knife
Spatula
Square baking pan
Wooden spoons

Good morning, dear

Starting Off Right

Breakfast in "A Canyon, Colorado Diner"
a counter-style starter for 6

*The love remembered as most sweet is the one
we never again will meet.*

Awaitress and a wandering man. Ian Tyson's classic "Navajo Rug," (written with celebrated songwriter Tom Russell) sings to the sentimental memory of a tender, lost love—Katie, a diner waitress.

All that's left is a sweet melancholy recalled in textile shades of red and blue. "I saw lightning 'cross the sacred mountains," Tyson sings, "Saw woven turtle doves." The lovers, like a Navajo rug's woven storyline, are forever wound together by the sweet strands of time. The diner's gone, but their long-lost love, anchored by the storyteller's memory of "lying next to Katie on that old Navajo rug," lives on. "It's hard," the singer knows, "to find things that last any more" like true love or "an old woven Navajo."

In dreamlike memory, Katie serves her coffee-shop lover "two eggs up on whiskey toast." THE WHISKEY TOAST or rye-bread recipe below is a sourdough-style tangy loaf tempered by rich, dark molasses with an intoxicating aroma and chewy, barely crisp crust.

A diner favorite, "home fries on the side" is a delicious way to use up dinner's baked potatoes. I first sampled this breakfast delight recklessly thrown together by the short order cook at Kate's Cafe (no relation to Tyson's waitress), a waterfront shack with terrific greasy-spoon food and several inches of atmosphere in the corners. My version of Kate's hash-browned Idaho flowers are seasoned with stories of small-town roadhouses and corner diners, where cowboys and truckers still court spirited waitresses.

Remember sweet days long past and silently drink a "roadhouse coffee" toast to cowboys (or waitresses) you once loved.

"Ay Yi Yi, Katie, Whatever became of the Navajo rug and you?"

Phrases in quotes are from "Navajo Rug" by Ian Tyson ©1986 Slick Fork Music—CAPAC and Tom Russell ©End of the Trail Music—CAPAC. Included on Tyson's award-winning album, Cowboyography.

Ham Steaks and Red-Eye Gravy

4 tablespoons vegetable oil
2 pounds ham steak (approximately),
   cut into 6 portions
3 tablespoons flour
1½ cups strong coffee

1 cup water
1½ tablespoons brown sugar
Salt and pepper to taste
Dash of mace
¼ cup half-and-half (optional)

1. Heat oil in a heavy skillet. Pepper ham steaks and fry each side until just browned.
2. Remove steaks; hold in warm oven. Pour out all but 3 tablespoons of drippings. Add flour to pan drippings and cook until thick, stirring constantly with a fork.
3. Slowly add coffee, stirring constantly. While still stirring, add water until gravy has thinned to desired consistency.
4. Add brown sugar, salt and pepper to taste, a dash of mace. Mix well, and stir until sugar is dissolved. If desired, mix in half-and-half.
5. Stir until heated through and pour over warm ham steaks.

Morning Home Fries

4 tablespoons olive oil
1 medium onion, chopped
6 large baked potatoes, cut in large cubes
½ teaspoon salt
½ teaspoon black pepper
1 teaspoon garlic powder
1 teaspoon paprika

1. Heat oil in heavy skillet, add onions and cook, stirring often, until translucent.
2. Add potatoes and mix well, coating them in the oil. Add spices.
3. Mix skillet often so potatoes and onions are coated with the spices, and the edges get barely brown.

VARIATION: For an easy, one-pan breakfast add crumbled bacon or cooked ham, crack eggs on top, cover with shredded cheese, and bake at 350 degrees until the yolks are firm and the cheese is soft and melted.

Frycakes, Fritters, Sinkers, Twisters:
Tips for Homemade Diner-style Donuts

Light raised centers with smooth, cake crusts take some practice. Don't be discouraged. The cakes themselves will be your guide. Browned crust and runny centers? The oil's too hot. Cold oil's to blame for greasy shells. Frycakes aren't much good the next day, so make the right amount for your crowd (although leftovers added to sweet bread pudding make a nice touch). True, homemade doughnuts can be a chore, but the reward of batter-bowls full of sweet, warm sinkers is more than worth the dusting of flour on your nose.

Spice Frycakes

4 cups flour
½ cup sugar
2 teaspoons baking soda
1 teaspoon baking powder
½ teaspoon salt
¼ teaspoon nutmeg
½ teaspoon allspice
¼ teaspoon mace
1 tablespoon dried orange peel
Dash ground cloves

2 teaspoons vanilla extract
3 tablespoons butter, melted
3 eggs, beaten
1 cup buttermilk

For dusting

1 cup sugar
½ teaspoon cinnamon

Melted vegetable shortening or light oil for frying

1. In a large bowl, combine flour, soda, powder, salt, and spices. Mix until well blended.
2. In a separate bowl, beat together melted butter, eggs, buttermilk, and vanilla.
3. Add liquid all at once to the flour mixture and stir until barely mixed.
4. Turn the dough out onto a lightly floured board and knead lightly until flour is mixed in. Don't over-handle the dough; 30 seconds should about do it.
5. Roll dough to ½ inch thick and cut with 3-inch donut cutter.
6. Melt shortening in a deep, heavy pot or Dutch oven. The oil should fill the pan to about 1 inch from the top. Heat fat over medium-high heat until a cube of bread browns in one minute or thermometer registers 375 degrees.
7. Slide cut donuts into hot oil, a few at a time. When they reach the surface, turn and cook until golden brown, turn again and cook until other side is browned.
8. Remove from oil and drain briefly on paper towels. Dust lightly with cinnamon sugar mixture.
9. Serve warm with plenty of fresh, hot coffee.

"Whiskey Toast" Beer Bread

2 cups flour

1½ cups rye flour

1 tablespoon baking powder

1 tablespoon caraway seeds

1 12-ounce can warm beer (dark is best)

1 egg, beaten

¼ cup molasses

2 tablespoons butter, melted

1. Preheat oven to 325 degrees. Oil or spray a 10-inch Dutch oven or cake pan.
2. In a large mixing bowl combine flours, caraway seeds, and baking powder.
3. In another bowl, beat together warm beer, egg, and molasses.
4. Pour beer mixture into flour and stir until a sticky dough forms.
5. Bake for 40 minutes.
6. Remove from oven and brush top with melted butter. Return to oven for 5 minutes or until crust is golden brown and bread is cooked through. It should make a hollow thud when rapped underneath.

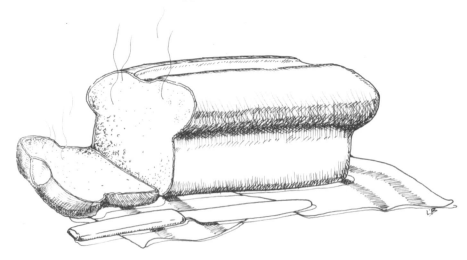

Waiting Together for the Thaw
a comforting morning meal for hearty appetites

A house is where a man lives, a home where he loves.

The West lies quietly beneath a picturesque mantle of snow. Line riders and camp men pull on leggings, buckle spurs to snow boots, and button up overcoats. Ranch wives, standing on the pick-up bed bouncing across open pastures, drop hay and cake to the hungry herd. By midmorning the countryside is crossed with dark, thick lines of cattle munching contentedly. Weary ranchmen, grateful for the extra help, head home for a warm breakfast.

Deep tracks call for teamwork. The great joy and lasting beauty of the family ranch is the strength of loving hands working together against seemingly impossible and unpredictable hardships. This is no town romance of hothouse flowers and sugar candy, but the warmth and security that comes from knowing you are not only loved but needed.

Invite summer into your kitchen with a breakfast menu flavored by New Mexico's warm sunshine.

Green chiles, extra mild or fiery hot, may be the Southwest's greatest contribution to American cooking. Though the canned variety are tasty, there is no real substitute for the rich, earthy tang of fresh-roasted New Mexico chiles. See the Sources section for information on a mail-order harvest.

The perfect complement to creamy, stuffed green chiles, SWEET POTATO PANCAKES are nutty, fragrant, and delicious topped with sour cream and applesauce. Teamed with SWEET BREAKFAST CORN BREAD, hot from the oven, and a slightly sour Texas-style fruit salad, you'll feel warm inside counting snowflakes together.

Cattlemen and cowhands, ranch wives and cowgirls look through the bleak weather, waiting for mother nature's warming chinook. Water rushes where just hours before there was ice, and for a few days the sheer delight of spring is tendered to the grateful outback.

Chili Relleno Eggs with Stewed-Tomato Sauce

2 4-ounce cans whole green chiles, or
   8 fresh roasted
2 cups Monterey jack cheese, grated
6 eggs

2 cups milk
½ teaspoon nutmeg
1½ tablespoons butter
1 tablespoon flour

1. Preheat oven to 325 degrees.
2. Slit each chili down one side and fill loosely with grated cheese, using one cup of cheese for all the chiles. Lay filled chiles in lightly buttered ovenproof casserole dish or shallow bowl.
3. In a separate bowl, beat eggs and 1 tablespoon flour, then mix in milk and nutmeg. When blended well, fold in the grated cheese.
4. Pour egg mixture over filled chiles, dot with butter, and bake for 45 minutes to 1 hour, until top is bubbly and knife inserted near center comes out clean.
5. Spoon Stewed-Tomato Sauce over eggs for serving.

Stewed-Tomato Sauce

2 16-ounce cans stewed tomatoes
1 teaspoon garlic
1 teaspoon basil flakes
1 tablespoon parsley flakes
½ teaspoon onion powder

½ teaspoon salt
¼ teaspoon black pepper
¼ teaspoon allspice
2 tablespoons butter

1. Combine all ingredients in a medium saucepan.
2. Simmer over medium heat for 15 to 20 minutes, until heated through.

Sweet-Potato Pancakes

2 large sweet potatoes, peeled and grated
1 pear or apple, grated
4 eggs, beaten
9 crackers (Ritz or other butter crackers,
    or saltines), crumbled to fine meal

½ teaspoon salt
¾ teaspoon nutmeg
¾ teaspoon cinnamon
Dash of black pepper
Light oil for frying

1. Mix all the ingredients, except for the oil, in a large bowl until well blended.
2. Pour oil to ¼ inch deep in heavy skillet and place over medium-high heat until very hot but not smoking. Oil should sizzle when a drop of water hits the pan.
3. Drop sweet-potato batter into hot oil by rounded tablespoonfuls. Fry on each side until golden brown. Repeat with remaining batter, adding more oil to pan if necessary. Serve with applesauce.

Citrus Slices With Poppy-Seed Dressing

For the dressing
½ cup mayonnaise
½ cup buttermilk
¼ cup sugar
¼ teaspoon salt
¼ medium red onion, grated
½ tablespoon prepared Dijon mustard

1 tablespoon poppy seeds
1 tablespoon lemon juice

Fruit
3 grapefruit
2 oranges

1. Combine all the ingredients for the dressing, mix until well blended.
2. Chill dressing at least 2 to 3 hours (overnight is best) before serving.
3. Peel fruits. With a knife, remove as much of the white membrane as possible.
4. Cut fruits across segments into ¼-inch-thick slices. Arrange on a serving platter and drizzle with prepared dressing. (Store leftover dressing in the refrigerator up to 2 weeks. It's also dandy on spinach or any green salad.)

Sweet Breakfast Corn Bread

½ cup golden raisins
¼ cup brandy or brandy extract (optional)
1¼ cups flour
1½ cups white cornmeal
2 teaspoons baking powder

¾ cup sugar
¼ teaspoon salt
2 eggs, beaten
1 cup milk
8 tablespoons butter, melted

1. Preheat oven to 350 degrees. Oil or spray a 7 x 11 baking pan.
2. Sprinkle brandy over the raisins and allow to soak while you mix the batter.
3. In a mixing bowl, combine dry ingredients, add beaten eggs and milk, and stir until well mixed. Add raisins, drained from remaining brandy.
4. Stir in melted butter until just mixed.
5. Pour batter into pan. Bake for 35 to 40 minutes, or until a knife inserted in center comes out clean.

VARIATION: Instead of raisins, when the batter is in the pan, stir in ½ cup of your favorite jelly or jam (you may need to heat it a bit to make it workable). Marble the jam through the bread. Don't mix it in; leave it in streaks through the batter. Bake as directed above.

He Feeds, I Cook
an easy meal for 4 hungry ranch hands

Keep your eyes wide open before marriage,
half shut afterwards. —Benjamin Franklin

Ask a ranch wife about her morning routine and you're likely to hear, "He feeds, I cook."

At the first break of daylight, he may be winding through the barn stalls feeding the colts he'll ride that day or throwing flakes of deep green hay to heavy cows waiting in the calving yards. In the house, the dogs are fed, supper's beans are slowly bubbling. She rushes: it's forty miles over rough dirt roads to her job in town.

Through the kitchen window she spies her husband washing off the pickup's muddy windshield. She hurries breakfast to the table and calls him inside.

On days when time runs short and breakfast is a hold-in-your-hand bite on the run, forget the drive-through and wrap up one of these lightly battered toast sandwiches with your choice of sweet or savory filling. It's an easy traveling meal—on horseback or rolling down the interstate.

Subtly spiced and just faintly sweet, tasty BREAKFAST SAUSAGE is easily made from ingredients on hand. It's terrific sliced into patties and panfried or served as a simple meat filling baked in crisp, tart apple halves.

HOMESTEADER HASH-BROWN PIE is a tasty legacy from a quieter time when we imagine wood-fired ovens cradled fresh yeast breads and picturesque double-fruit pies. Fostered by sweeping stories of prairie life and overland trails, we all seem to believe there are no hardships that can't be conquered by a loving family gathered around that trusty kitchen hearth.

Altough my grandmothers were wonderful cooks, it was at my mother's table that I learned my most important kitchen lesson…there is always room for one more. Smile warmly towards the extra place at your table and say, "You're always welcome here."

Mexicali Salsa Toast

8 slices bread (sourdough, French, or Italian style)
4 tablespoons cream cheese, softened to room temperature
4 teaspoons salsa
3 eggs, beaten
1 tablespoon warm water
1 tablespoon Parmesan cheese
1 teaspoon dried basil
1 teaspoon cilantro flakes
Salt and pepper to taste
3 tablespoons butter

1. Spread each slice of bread (on one side) with a thin layer (approximately ½ tablespoon) of cream cheese. Take care not to tear the bread.
2. Top the cream cheese on 4 of the slices with 1 teaspoon salsa each, cover with remaining 4 slices—cream-cheese sides together, making "salsa sandwiches."
3. Beat together eggs, water, cheese, basil, cilantro, salt, and pepper.
4. Melt butter in skillet or griddle, quickly dip both sides of "salsa sandwiches" in egg mixture and place in hot skillet. Fry each side until golden brown.
5. Repeat with remaining sandwiches, adding more butter to skillet if necessary.

Cowboy's Sweetheart Sugar Toast

8 slices bread (honey wheat, French, or
    sourdough)
4 tablespoons cream cheese
4 teaspoons jam or orange marmalade
3 eggs, beaten

2 tablespoons milk
1 teaspoon vanilla extract
½ teaspoon cinnamon
3 tablespoons butter
Powdered sugar for dusting

1. Spread each slice of bread (on one side) with a thin layer (approximately ½ tablespoon) of cream cheese. Take care not to tear the bread.
2. Top the cream cheese on 4 of the slices with 1 teaspoon jam each, cover with remaining 4 slices—cream cheese sides together, making "sweet sandwiches."
3. Beat together eggs, milk, cinnamon and vanilla.
4. Melt butter in skillet or griddle, quickly dip both sides of "sweet sandwiches" in egg mixture and place in hot skillet. Fry until golden brown and warm in the center, turn over, and again fry until golden brown.
5. Repeat with remaining sandwiches; add more butter to skillet if necessary.
6. Dust with powdered sugar and serve.

Breakfast Sausage

½ pound ground pork
1½ tablespoons apple sauce
½ tablespoon brown sugar
⅛ teaspoon thyme
⅛ teaspoon allspice

Rounded ¼ teaspoon rubbed sage
Dash of cayenne pepper
¼ teaspoon salt
⅛ teaspoon black pepper

1. Combine all ingredients in a large bowl and knead until well blended.
2. Roll into a log about 3 inches in diameter. Refrigerate overnight.
3. Slice and panfry in lightly oiled skillet, or follow recipe for *Savory Stuffed Apples*.

Savory Stuffed Apples

2 tart apples
½ pound pork sausage or 1 recipe
  Breakfast Sausage

1½ teaspoons bread crumbs
Dash of mace

1. Preheat oven to 350 degrees.
2. Cut apples in half and core, being careful not to break the skin.
3. Remove ½ to ⅔ of the apple pulp, chop, and knead into sausage.
4. Stuff each apple half with one ¼ of the sausage mixture.
5. Sprinkle each stuffed apple half with bread crumbs and a dash of mace.
6. Bake for 60 to 75 minutes, until apples are soft and sausage is cooked through.

Note: The pan juices from this dish make a particularly delicious gravy.

VARIATION: Stack sausage patties and thick apple slices in a casserole. Bake as directed.

Homesteader Hash-Brown Pie

6 medium potatoes
1 medium onion
2 eggs
½ cup grated cheese (mozzarella, jack, or cheddar)

½ cup sour cream
1 teaspoon salt
¼ teaspoon pepper
½ teaspoon garlic powder
⅛ teaspoon nutmeg

1. Preheat oven to 350 degrees.
2. Shred potatoes and onion into a mixing bowl. Add remaining ingredients and mix well.
3. Pour batter into lightly greased large skillet or casserole dish.
4. Bake for 60 to 75 minutes, until top is crunchy and potatoes are cooked.

Hearty Fruit Salad

2 bananas, peeled and thickly sliced
2 sweet red apples, cored and diced
2 pears, cored and diced
1 small bunch (about ½ pound) seedless grapes, removed from stems
1 cup dark raisins

16 ounces vanilla yogurt
3 tablespoons table cream
1 tablespoon brown sugar
½ teaspoon nutmeg
4 ounces slivered or sliced almonds

1. Mix fruit and almonds in large serving bowl; toss well.
2. In a separate bowl, blend together remaining ingredients and pour over prepared fruit.
3. Fold fruit into the sauce until completely coated.
4. Refrigerate until ready to serve.

On the Job Before Daylight
breakfast for a hungry family of 4 to 6 hands

Be good and you will be lonesome. —Mark Twain

Morning comes early in ranch country; days start well before dawn. In summer, when light is long, the extra time offers a head start on a full day of chores. But in winter, those early hours mean hearty breakfasts, pots of coffee, and eager hands waiting for enough light to begin work. The kids may lay abed just a bit longer, leaving you time for quiet conversation and simple togetherness. Start off right with a simply prepared breakfast they'll remember through the day's circles and appreciate even longer.

FRESH SALSA, a gift from south of the border, is a delicious blend of summer's bounty. Keep it ready to top roasted meats, eggs, and trusty tortilla chips. In winter, when fresh tomatoes are disappointing at best, I settle for big-city salsas in jars, but while fruits are red on the vine, there is always a batch of garden fresh *pico de gallo* chilling in the fridge.

This version, made extra tangy with brilliant green tomatillos, is a modern variation sure to keep the gringos happy.

Puffy and golden brown, BROILED OMELETTES are the perfect spot to hide leftover vegetables or even cooked meats. Wrapped in warm buttered tortillas, any combination of fillings you favor will bring shining morning smiles.

GOOD MORNING CANNED-FRUIT CAKE is my old standby. It's an east-as-ready-made, drop-in-for-coffee-anytime, spur-of-the-moment sweet. When shelves have seemed barest, I've topped the simple batter with canned peaches, pears, figs, or even lonely, leftover whole-berry cranberry sauce. Serve thick wedges right from the hot skillet.

As early morning light slowly fills the sky, send him off with a full stomach and a warm heart.

Broiled Omelette

2 tablespoons butter
½ onion, chopped
3 Roma tomatoes or ½ large tomato,
    sliced
½ green pepper, chopped
5 mushrooms, sliced
¾ to 1 cup canned or frozen (defrosted)
    corn kernels

1 baked potato
½ teaspoon salt
¼ teaspoon pepper
1 teaspoon basil flakes
6 eggs, beaten
1 cup shredded cheese (cheddar,
    Monterey jack, or mixed)

1. Preheat oven to broil.
2. In an ovenproof skillet, sauté onion in butter. When onions are translucent,
   add remaining vegetables and spices. Cook until just tender.
3. Pour eggs into skillet, stirring to coat all the vegetables. Top with shredded
   cheese, and cook just 3 to 4 minutes more, until eggs are set on the sides but
   still runny in the center of the pan.
4. Place skillet under broiler for 5 minutes, until top is puffy and golden brown.

Buttered Tortillas

Preheat oven to 350 degrees. Stack your choice of flour or corn tortillas with a thin
sliver of butter in the center of each bread. For a Mexicali breakfast sweet, sprinkle
butter with cinnamon and sugar mixture. For a savory taste, top butter with a dash
of parsley flakes, chili powder, and Tabasco. Wrap the entire stack securely in tin
foil, and bake on the center rack for 10 to 12 minutes, until butter is melted and
tortillas are warmed throughout.

Breakfast Refritos (Refried Beans)

½ pound bacon
½ onion, minced
1 16-ounce can black beans, drained
½ jalapeño (fresh or canned), seeded and
  minced
¼ teaspoon salt

¼ teaspoon garlic powder
1 teaspoon cilantro flakes
½ loosely packed cup shredded cheese
  (Monterey or pepper jack, feta,
  sharp Swiss, or mix cheddar and jack)

1. Fry bacon over medium heat until about half cooked.
2. Add onion and cook until bacon is crisp.
3. Remove bacon and add remaining ingredients (except for cheese). While cooking 10 to 15 minutes longer (to meld flavors), mash beans with the back of a spoon to form a thick paste.
4. Arrange bacon around edges of skillet, sprinkle center with shredded cheese, and cover. Heat just long enough to melt cheese. Watch carefully that beans don't burn at this stage.

Fresh Salsa

1 pound (about 2 cups) tomatoes, diced
4 canned tomatillos, chopped
1 bunch green onions, chopped
½ cup fresh cilantro leaves, chopped

3 tablespoons lime juice
1–3 serrano chiles, minced
1 teaspoon garlic powder

1. Combine all the ingredients in a mixing bowl and toss well.
2. Refrigerate until ready to serve.

VARIATION: For an unusual salsa, add 1 to 2 ounces crumbled feta cheese or a chopped avocado.

Broiled Grapefruit

2 to 3 grapefruit (½ per person)
2 to 3 tablespoons butter each, melted
4 to 6 tablespoons brown sugar

1. Preheat oven to broil.
2. Cut grapefruit in half around its girth. With a sharp knife, trace the outline of the fruit to loosen segments.
3. Brush each top with approximately ½ tablespoon butter.
4. Sprinkle each with a tablespoon of brown sugar.
5. Broil for 2 to 3 minutes, until sugar melts and bubbles on top.

Good Morning Canned-Fruit Cake

1 stick butter, softened
1 cup plus 3 tablespoons sugar
½ cup brown sugar
2 eggs, beaten
2 teaspoons vanilla
2 cups flour
2 tablespoons baking powder

1 teaspoon baking soda
½ teaspoon salt
1¼ cups buttermilk
1 large can (14 to 20 ounces) fruit
  (peaches, pears, fruit cocktail, or
  berries), drained
½ teaspoon cinnamon

1. Preheat oven to 350 degrees. Oil or spray a 10- to 11-inch skillet.
2. Cream butter, 1 cup sugar, and brown sugar. Add eggs, vanilla and mix well.
3. In a separate bowl, mix dry ingredients, except for cinnamon and remaining sugar.
4. Add flour mixture alternately with buttermilk, beating well after each addition until batter is thick and smooth.
5. Pour batter into skillet, arrange drained fruit on top of batter, and bake for 25 minutes.
6. Combine remaining sugar and cinnamon. After 25 minutes, sprinkle cake top with sugar mixture and return to oven for 5 to 10 minutes, until a knife inserted in center comes out clean.

Hungry
by noon

Western Dinners and Lunchtime Treats

A Saddlebag Secret
a picnic lunch for 4 to 6

Good husbands are made by good wives.

Gathering the herd, you are searching together through the rocky arroyos and heavy brush of distant pastures. Running after strays, there's no time to ride in for a mid-day meal. When he's alone, a quick candy bar or extra morning biscuit tucked away in pocket or saddlebag has to hold him until the day's work is over.

Make the most of your time together, even if your morning is shared with bawling cattle and swinging ropes. Hide away a saddlebag secret. Around noon, when he starts to reach for a handy snack, reach instead for your picnic-on-the-go.

If there's time, spread a cheery gingham cloth and unpack napkins, plates, forks, knives, and a Thermos of hot coffee. With cattle to move, there's no time to waste; your picnic could easily become a horseback treat.

STUFFED CACKLEBERRIES, an easy finger food, are a hit with on-the-go eaters, young and old. GINGER-HONEY FLANK STEAK, delicious warm or cold, is a simple way to whoop up familiar fare. Slice thin across the grain and serve as lively sandwiches or in a tangy beef salad.

Potato salad, though it's difficult to balance on the saddle horn, is worth the extra effort. No food is so laden with the nostalgia of sunny days, country fairs, and spring love as this venerable favorite.

EXTRA-MOIST PANNIER LOAF, inspired by old-time potato yeast breads, can wait for hours and still stay moist and chewy. It's the perfect bread to take down the trail for homemade flavor, no matter how far from home. Soft and slightly sweet, APPLES AND OATS COOKIES pack well and look good enough to eat even after a bumpy ride to town.

With this delicious lunch, be prepared to catch more than one hungry cowboy.

Stuffed Cackleberries

6 eggs
3 tablespoons mayonnaise
1 tablespoon sour cream
¼ teaspoon salt
¼ teaspoon dry mustard

⅛ teaspoon dill
⅛ teaspoon paprika
Dash of cayenne pepper
Dash of black pepper
Paprika for dusting

1. In a small saucepan, cover eggs with cold water and boil for 10 minutes over medium heat. Drain, cover with cold water, and let cool before peeling.
2. Carefully cut the peeled eggs in half, lengthwise. Remove the yolks to a small mixing bowl. Reserve the whites.
3. Mash the yolks with the tines of a fork. Add remaining ingredients and stir into a thick paste.
4. Fill 6 of the egg-white halves with the yolk mixture, then top with the remaining whites to form "whole" eggs. Dust lightly with paprika, and refrigerate.

Ginger-Honey Flank Steak

1 2-pound flank steak or London broil
2 tablespoons butter, softened
½ cup honey
¼ cup stone-ground mustard

½ teaspoon powdered ginger
⅛ teaspoon cayenne pepper
Salt and black pepper

1. Preheat oven to broil.
2. Make a thick paste of the butter, honey, mustard, ginger, and cayenne pepper.
3. Rub top of steak with half of seasoning paste. Broil 5 minutes for medium rare, or longer, depending on your taste.
4. Turn steak and top with remaining mixture. Add salt and pepper to taste, broil 5 minutes or longer, depending on your preference.
5. Slice across the grain. Serve cold or at room temperature.

Extra-Moist Pannier Loaf

1 medium potato or 1 cup leftover
   mashed potatoes
1 cup buttermilk
2 teaspoons baking powder

1 teaspoon baking soda
1 ½ teaspoons rosemary leaves (optional)
1 teaspoon salt
2 ¼ cups flour

1. Preheat oven to 375 degrees. Oil or spray loaf pan.
2. Peel and cut potato into large cubes. Place in small saucepan, cover with cold water, and boil over medium-high heat for 15 to 20 minutes, until tender but not mushy.
3. Mash soft potatoes until smooth. Allow them to come to room temperature before proceeding with recipe.
4. Transfer potatoes to large mixing bowl. Heat buttermilk till it is warm but not scalding, add to potatoes, and stir until well blended.
5. Mix in baking powder, soda, rosemary, and salt. Add flour, mix until just blended.
6. On a lightly floured surface, knead dough until smooth and elastic.
7. Shape dough into a loaf and place in large, lightly greased loaf pan. Bake for 50 to 60 minutes on center rack, until top is golden brown and loaf sounds hollow when tapped underneath.

Picnic Potato Salad

8 medium potatoes
4 stalks celery, chopped
1 medium red onion, chopped
½ green bell pepper, seeded and
   chopped
1 6-ounce can black olives, drained
1 teaspoon garlic powder
1 teaspoon salt
½ teaspoon black pepper

1 tablespoon parsley flakes
1 tablespoon basil leaves
½ teaspoon paprika
Pinch of cayenne pepper
¾ cup mayonnaise
½ cup sour cream
1½ tablespoons prepared mustard
1 tablespoon cider vinegar
¼ cup cream

1. Cover potatoes in a stockpot with cold water and set to boil over medium heat for 20 minutes, or until cooked through but not mushy.
2. Drain potatoes and allow to cool. Peel if desired, cut into bite-sized pieces, and place in large mixing bowl.
3. Add chopped vegetables and spices, and toss well.
4. In a separate bowl, blend together mayonnaise, sour cream, mustard, vinegar, and cream.
5. Pour over vegetables and spices, folding in until vegetables are well coated.

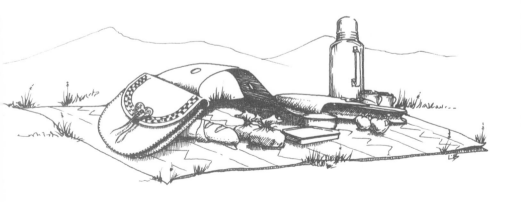

Apples and Oats Cookies

½ cup butter-flavored vegetable shortening
1 cup brown sugar
1 cup sugar
1 egg
1 cup unsweetened applesauce
1 teaspoon baking soda
½ teaspoon baking powder
½ teaspoon salt

½ teaspoon cinnamon
¼ teaspoon nutmeg
2 cups flour
3 cups old-fashioned oatmeal (not quick-cooking)
1 cup raisins
1½ cups chopped walnuts or pecans

1. Preheat oven to 350 degrees.
2. In a large mixing bowl, cream shortening and sugars. Add egg, applesauce, soda, powder, salt, cinnamon, and nutmeg. Mix until well blended.
3. Mix in flour and oatmeal. Add raisins and nuts and stir until well blended.
4. Drop rounded tablespoonfuls onto an ungreased cookie sheet. Bake for 12 to 15 minutes.
5. Cool on wire racks.

Note: This is a slightly soft, chewy cookie, with almost puffed, rounded tops. Bake only until brown, and allow to cool slightly before removing from cookie sheets.

The Preacher Comes To Call
an early supper for 4 to 6

Love looks with the eyes but sees with the heart.

Ladies in flowered spring dresses and men in starched white shirts drift down the stone steps. Children run happily by. Each in turn stops to visit with the soft-spoken man in black.

"See you after a bit, Pastor John," you smile warmly. Catching a glimpse of your sparkling new stone, you add, "Supper's just about ready."

Later, shaking the light rain off his coat, he beams, "Let's see about setting that date." The preacher, sitting at your mother's table, sharing the first company meal you've cooked alone, has come to discuss the ceremony.

SMOTHERED YARDBIRD so easily creates tender, delicately seasoned meat surrounded by truly luscious white gravy that you'll pardon its use of modern conveniences like tinned soup. It's just right ladled over CORN DODGERS, an up-dated version of the chewy bread once a staple on frontier tables.

Not so long ago out on the wild plains, far from supermarkets and office jobs, precious white flour was often saved for special occasions. With the bottom of the barrel in sight, homestead mothers and wagon cooks adapted recipes from Native American fires. Cornmeal, perhaps with nothing more than cool water, became everything from crusty breads to griddle-fried cakes.

Little-known in northern cow counties, stewed greens are a deliciously bitter southern tradition. Gently simmered, the pungent flavor mellows to a pleasant, peppery sensation that dances across your taste buds. Serve the greens covered by their cooking liquid, or use that "likker" (rumored to cure a variety of ills) as the base for homemade soup.

Though not all cowboys are southern, this distinctive Dixie menu tips its hat to the many who came with loaded wagon, pack horse, or simple carpet bag to work and claim the vast western lands.

Corn Dodgers (Hot-Water Corn Bread)

Recipe makes 10 panfried corn cakes

1 cup cornmeal
2 teaspoons baking powder
3 tablespoons flour
1 teaspoon salt
3 teaspoons sugar

1 egg, well beaten
½–¾ cup milk
1 cup boiling water
Vegetable oil for the griddle

1. Pour boiling water over cornmeal and stir until well mixed.
2. When cornmeal has cooled a bit, add the rest of the dry ingredients alternating with the milk and egg. Mixture should be the consistency of pancake batter.
3. Ladle batter into 4- to 5-inch cakes on a hot griddle coated with vegetable oil over medium-high heat. Cook until edges are set and bubbles appear and begin to break, and cakes are golden brown. Flip and cook through on other side.

Note: Remember to keep the griddle well oiled while frying the remaining cakes. Let cooked johnnycakes rest in a 150- to 200-degree oven. It won't hurt the chicken any to wait in the oven while you finish the bread.

VARIATION: For a richer, thicker corn bread, substitute buttermilk for milk in this recipe. For buttermilk corn dodgers, use ½ teaspoon baking soda and 1 teaspoon baking powder instead of amounts specified here.

Smothered Yardbird

1 frying chicken cut into 8 pieces
1 cup flour
2 teaspoons poultry seasoning
½ teaspoon garlic powder (to taste)
½ teaspoon onion powder
½ cup buttermilk (See substitution)
1 cup vegetable shortening or oil for frying

2–4 baking potatoes
2 carrots, peeled (optional)
1 onion, sliced thin and separated
1 can cream of mushroom soup
1 can cream of chicken soup
1 soup can water
Salt and pepper to taste

1. Preheat oven to 300 degrees.
2. Combine flour, poultry seasoning, garlic powder, and onion powder.
3. Dip each chicken piece in buttermilk and coat well with flour mixture.
4. Melt shortening over medium-high heat until hot and water sprinkled in the pan sizzles.
5. Shake extra flour from chicken and fry 3 to 4 pieces at a time until lightly browned on all sides.
6. Transfer pieces to a large baking pan; a chicken roaster is perfect.
7. Slice potatoes and carrots about ¼ to ½ inch thick and fry quickly in the same oil until outsides are crisp, but not cooked all the way through. Remove with slotted spoon and add to chicken in roaster.
8. Pour out all but 2 tablespoons of the oil, add onion, and cook until just soft.
9. Combine soups and water; add to pan and stir until mixed and warm.
10. Pour soup and onions over the chicken and vegetables.
11. Bake for 2½ to 3 hours, until meat is tender and gravy is bubbling.

Substitution: In place of buttermilk, you can substitute sweet milk, or 1 egg, or leftover egg whites beaten with 2 tablespoons water.

Note: You may choose to cover the meat in the oven if it will be unattended for much of the cooking time or if the gravy starts to develop a tough surface. Cover for half of cooking time or, occasionally, simply stir the meat down into the gravy.

Mess O' Greens

¼ pound salt pork (fatback)
2 bunches fresh greens (collard, mustard, turnip, or beet)

1 medium onion, chopped
6 cups chicken stock

1. Peel the rind from salt pork and cut into cubes.
2. Wash greens thoroughly in a sink or basin filled with cold water to remove sand.
3. Tear hard stems from greens and rip leaves into large pieces.
4. In a heavy stockpot, sauté salt pork and onions, stirring often until onions are just translucent. Pour in chicken stock, add greens, and bring to a boil.
5. Reduce heat to simmer and allow to cook 4 to 5 hours, or longer if desired. Longer cooking mellows but does not diminish the peppery flavor. Greens should be tender but not mushy to bite.

Guidelines for Great Beans

1. Always add warm water to cooking beans; cold water will make them tough.
2. If the beans begin to scorch, either remove, without stirring, to another pot or dissolve 2 tablespoons sugar in warm water and add to beans. Don't worry, the sweet taste will cook out.
3. If the liquid becomes too salty, add a whole potato. When the salt taste has cleared, remove and discard the potato.
4. Don't be afraid of cooking too long or adding too much water. The longer beans cook, the better.
5. If you're ready to serve and the cooking liquid is still too thin, take ½ cup of beans with ½ cup of liquid, purée in blender, return to pot, and stir in well.

All-Day Red Beans

1 pound red beans
2 large chicken bouillon cubes
1 onion, cut in quarters
3 cloves garlic, peeled
2 stalks celery
1 tablespoon worcestershire sauce

½–1 teaspoon canned roasted diced
  jalapénos (to taste)
2 tablespoons cilantro flakes
1 tablespoon parsley flakes
Salt and black pepper to taste
Water

1. Wash and pick over beans for rocks, twigs, bad beans, etc.
2. Cover beans in water (by at least 3 to 4 inches) and let rest overnight. If you are cooking beans in an iron pot, let them soak in a kitchen bowl. Otherwise, set them to soak right in your cooking vessel. Instead of soaking, you may bring beans and 3 quarts water to a rolling boil on the stove, remove from heat and let stand for one hour.
3. To prepare beans, add or discard enough water to cover beans by 2 inches.
4. Add remaining ingredients and bring to a boil.
5. Reduce heat to medium low, keep the water bubbling and the beans moving in the pot.
6. When celery starts to fall apart, remove it from pot and keep the beans on the stove until soft, tender, and flavorful—depending on your altitude this may take from 4 to 8 or even 10 hours. Don't worry. Just keep adding warm water so beans don't dry out and stir whenever you pass by (at least twice an hour, if possible). Keep tasting the liquid to adjust seasonings as needed.

Canned Peach Double-Fruit Cobbler

For the Filling

1 29-ounce can sliced peaches in syrup (or
    home-canned equivalent), drained,
    syrup reserved
2 tablespoons cornstarch
½ cup brown sugar
1 teaspoon cinnamon
½ teaspoon nutmeg
½ teaspoon allspice
1 tablespoon lemon juice
¼ cup reserved syrup
3 tablespoons butter

For the Crust

2 cups flour
½ cup sugar
1 teaspoon baking powder
1 teaspoon vanilla
1 cup of reserved peach syrup
1 stick of butter, melted

Sprinkle on Top

1 tablespoon sugar
½ teaspoon cinnamon

1. Preheat oven to 350 degrees.
2. In a Dutch oven or deep oven-to-table baking dish, combine all the ingredients for the filling except the butter. Toss until peaches are well coated with dry ingredients.
3. Dot the top of the peach filling with three tablespoons of butter cut into teaspoon-sized pieces.
4. In a separate bowl, mix flour, baking powder, and sugar for crust.
5. Mix in liquid ingredients and stir until a sticky dough has formed.
6. Spread dough over the peaches, being careful to reach the edges of the pan and to patch any holes so the filling stays sealed beneath.
7. Bake for 35 to 45 minutes, until crust is cooked through and peach filling is bubbling hot.

Hand Holding In The Parlor
a slow cooking supper for 4 to 6

Quiet times make charmed memories.

You've waited so long for a lazy afternoon together. Outside the wind whistles through bare trees, bringing down new showers of snow. Inside, homey and warm, the fire crackles and sparks invitingly.

There is perhaps nothing more romantic, nothing more nostalgic, nothing that makes a guest feel more special than the delicious scent of home-baked bread. Bake your bread in the morning, wrap it in a clean towel, and set aside. Rich and slightly sour, DUTCH-OVEN SODA BREAD only tastes better with time to rest and let the flavor mellow.

CREAMY BEAN SOUP, a rustic rendition of winter's favorite, patiently bubbles on the stove, waiting for one last game of hearts or for guests held up by drifting snow.

My mom's STOVE-TOP BRISKET, one of my father's favorite dishes, turns a tough cut into tender, melt-in-your-mouth beef that tastes even better the second day. To serve, spoon warm pan juices over thin slices of soda bread and top with the flavorful meat.

While supper's rich aroma fills the house, strum tunes on the guitar, tickle the ivories, or even read aloud. Sample cowboy poems by masters Badger Clark, Bruce Kiskaddon, S. Omar Barker, or Henry Herbert Knibbs and retell sweeping stories of wild lands.

Though the season may tempt you to hide behind shuttered windows, while supper's stewing, set aside the sugar dumpling dough, leave the brisket gently simmering, and bundle up for a leisurely stroll across frosted plains. Then come inside for dinner in the easy style of a simpler time.

Turn the lights down low.

Creamy Bean Soup

1 pound great northern beans
1 meaty ham bone or 2 ham hocks
1 large onion, chopped
2 bay leaves
1 28-ounce can whole tomatoes, chopped,
   with juice reserved
3 potatoes, cubed
3 carrots, cubed
2 stalks celery, chopped

3 tablespoons parsley flakes
½ teaspoon oregano
2 tablespoons lemon juice
1 large chicken bouillon cube
Salt and pepper to taste
2 cups half-and-half
2 teaspoons cornstarch mixed with 2
   teaspoons cold water

1. In stock pot, cover beans with water (by at least 2 inches) and soak overnight.
2. Add ham bone, enough water to cover beans by two inches, onion, and bay leaves, and boil slowly over medium heat about 2 hours, until beans are tender.
3. Remove bone and pour out water until beans are just covered by about 2 inches. Taste cooking water and season with salt and pepper to taste.
4. Cut meat from bone and return to pot. Add remaining ingredients, except for half-and-half and cornstarch mixture. Simmer until vegetables are tender, 1 to 1½ hours.
5. Just before serving, stir in half-and-half and cornstarch mixture. Re-season with salt and pepper, heat until thickened, and serve.

Dutch-oven Soda Bread

4 cups flour
2 teaspoons salt
1½ teaspoons baking soda

½ teaspoon baking powder
1¾ cups buttermilk

1. Preheat oven to 375 degrees. Oil or spray a 10- to 12- inch Dutch oven.
2. Combine flour, salt, soda, and powder, in a large bowl and mix well.
3. Add buttermilk and stir until mixed.
4. Turn dough out onto a lightly floured surface and knead until smooth, about 3 to 4 minutes.
5. Shape into round loaf and place in Dutch oven. With a sharp knife, cut a shallow cross in the top.
6. Bake for 50 minutes or until cross is spread, bread is browned, and it makes a hollow sound when thumped on the bottom.
7. Allow to cool completely on a wire rack before slicing and serving.

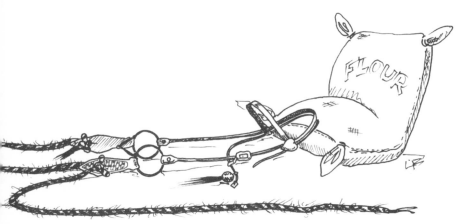

Stove-top Brisket

Approximately 2-pound beef brisket
2 teaspoons salt
1 teaspoon garlic powder
1 teaspoon pepper
1 teaspoon paprika

1 medium onion, sliced
4 pitted prunes
1 cup green beans, cleaned and snapped
    (fresh or frozen and defrosted)
⅔ cup water

1. Preheat oven to broil.
2. Combine spices and rub into both sides of meat.
3. Place meat, fat-side up, in ovenproof dish (with tight-fitting lid) that can go on the stove. Cook for 10 minutes, uncovered (on the rack farthest away from the heating element). Turn meat and cook 5 minutes more.
4. Remove from oven and add sliced onion and ⅔ cup of water. Place covered pan on stove over high heat until liquid begins to boil, then turn heat to low and cook 2 hours.
5. After 2 hours, add pitted prunes and cook on low heat, covered, for 1 hour and 40 minutes more.
6. Add green beans and cook for 20 minutes more.

Note: If desired, refrigerate cooked brisket overnight, then in the morning skim the excess fat from the broth and slice cold meat. When ready to serve, heat through in defatted cooking broth.

VARIATION: For a flavorful side dish, add quartered potatoes to the rich, brown liquid for the last 40 minutes of cooking time.

Stewed Fruit with Sugar Dumplings

1 8-ounce package dried peaches
1 6-ounce package dried apricots
1 6-ounce package dried apple chunks
1 12-ounce package prunes
1 cup raisins
3 cups apple juice

1 cup red wine
2 cinnamon sticks
1½ cups sugar
¾ cup brown sugar
1 tablespoon lemon peel
6 cups water

1. Combine all ingredients in a large, heavy-bottomed stockpot with tight cover.
2. Bring to a full boil over medium-high heat, then quickly reduce heat. Simmer, partially covered, for 1½ to 2 hours, until fruit is surrounded with a rich, thick sugar syrup.
3. Serve topped with fresh, heavy cream and Sugar Dumplings (recipe follows).

Sugar Dumplings

1 cup flour
1 cup sugar
1½ teaspoons baking powder
¼ teaspoon salt

4 tablespoons butter-flavored vegetable
*   shortening or butter, room temperature*
1 egg, beaten

1. In a large bowl, mix flour, sugar, baking powder, and salt.
2. Cut in shortening or butter until dough resembles a coarse meal. Blend in egg and set mixture aside.
3. Bring fruit in syrup to a boil, being careful not to burn the compote. Then drop batter by tablespoonfuls into the hot syrup.
4. When all the batter has been added, cover the pot tightly, reduce heat to low, and allow to simmer, without looking, for 12 minutes.
5. After 12 minutes, check the batter. It should be puffy and fairly dry. If necessary, replace lid and cook a few minutes longer.

Before the Barn Dance
a simple spread for 4 to 6 eager dancers

A loving heart is always young. —Greek Proverb

Two-step, polka, waltz, or swing—cowboys love to dance. Not the lonely combination of steps performed in lines to the latest Nashville craze, but tenderly whirling and spinning together to the heady strains of twin fiddles and Spanish guitars.

Lulled into a rhythm steady as the quarter horse's familiar gait, couples float above the floor whispering sweetly, wrapped in a velvet cloak of night. For young and old alike, this is cowboy romance.

If your two-step needs touching up, perhaps you could gently suggest a friendly trade: a few well-guided turns around a slick wood floor in exchange for a home-cooked meal before the next barn dance in town. Eat well but not too heavily. Be light on your feet.

Start with a warm bowl of CHUNKY TOMATO SOUP—hearty with just a delicate kiss of rich cream. Follow this lightly red ragout with a western version of an English favorite, COWBOY COTTAGE PIE. When the corn meal topping is golden brown and just dry throughout, the savory filling bubbles with the herbed aroma of a summer nights along the moor. Distant music hangs in the air.

For dessert, a near century-old American specialty, PINEAPPLE UPSIDE-DOWN CAKE is an easy, sweet treat baked in its own glossy frosting.

Though women have gained startling equality everywhere from the boardroom to the barnyard, on the dance floor the man must lead. And that, in our often too-modern age, is the great magic of the dance. Not the innocent way cheeks brush in time to the band, or a delightfully weary head resting on a stronger shoulder, but the unspoken agreement to trust in each other and follow another's sure-footed steps—a comfortable confidence that forges memorable dances and lasting relationships.

Chunky Tomato Soup

8 tablespoons butter
1 onion, chopped fine
1 clove garlic, minced
2 16-ounce cans diced tomatoes, drained,
    or 1 28-ounce can whole tomatoes,
    drained and diced
1 16-ounce can chicken broth
½ teaspoon sugar
1 teaspoon salt

¼ teaspoon pepper
2 bay leaves
1 teaspoon ground thyme
1 teaspoon basil flakes
1 tablespoon diced green chiles
2 teaspoons corn starch mixed with
    2 teaspoons cold water
½ cup milk
½ cup sour cream

1. In a medium-sized stockpot, sautée the onion and garlic in 4 tablespoons of butter.
2. Add tomatoes, chicken stock, spices, and green chiles. Cook, covered, for 45 minutes over medium heat.
3. If a smooth soup is desired, purée the cooked vegetable mixture in small batches in the blender. For chunky soup, add the cornstarch mixed with cold water to thicken the mixture and omit step 5.
4. Return puréed soup to saucepan. Over medium heat, stir in milk, sour cream, and remaining butter.
5. Heat until butter has melted; taste and re-season as desired. Serve.

Carrot Salad

1 pound carrots, peeled and shredded
1 cup raisins
½ cup chopped walnuts (optional)
¼ cup honey

½ cup mayonnaise
1 tablespoon cider vinegar
2 tablespoons applesauce (sweetened)
¼ teaspoon nutmeg

1. Toss carrots, walnuts, and raisins in a medium-size serving bowl.
2. In a small mixing bowl, combine remaining ingredients, and blend until well mixed.
3. Pour over carrots and raisins, tossing well to coat.
4. Refrigerate until ready to serve.

Cowboy Cottage Pie

For the Savory Filling

5 strips bacon, chopped

1 medium onion, chopped

1 pound ground beef (or leftover cooked
    meat cut into chunks)

3 tablespoons parsley flakes

2 cloves garlic, crushed

1 teaspoon nutmeg

½ green or red bell pepper, chopped

1 teaspoon paprika

½ teaspoon thyme

1 15-ounce can tomato sauce

⅓ cup beer

1 16-ounce can corn

1 16-ounce bag of frozen peas and carrots

Salt and pepper to taste

2 tablespoons cornstarch blended with 2
    tablespoons cold water

For the Cornmeal Topping

1½ cups cornmeal

1 cups flour

2 eggs

1 teaspoon soda

3 teaspoons baking powder

1 cup beer, reserve rest of can for filling

1 cup buttermilk

1 teaspoon salt

2 tablespoons sugar

¼ cup oil

1½ cups grated cheddar cheese

1. Preheat oven to 400 degrees. Butter or spray baking dish or two Dutch ovens.
2. In a saucepan, combine bacon, onions, and ground beef. Cook over medium heat until meat is well browned. If you are using cooked meat, add the meat when the onions have become soft.
3. Add remaining ingredients except for the corn, peas and carrots, and cornstarch. Allow to simmer 10 to 20 minutes so flavors can meld.
4. Stir in cornstarch, heat a few minutes more, stir in corn and frozen vegetables and transfer filling to baking dish.
5. In medium mixing bowl, combine the dry ingredients for cornmeal topping.
6. Add liquid ingredients and mix well. Fold in grated cheese.
7. Pour cornmeal batter over prepared meat filling. Bake for 30 to 40 minutes, until topping is golden brown and knife inserted in crust comes out clean.

Pineapple Upside-Down Cake

2 sticks butter
¾ cup brown sugar
2 8-ounce cans (8 slices) sliced pineapple
8 maraschino cherries (optional)
½ cup chopped pecans
1 cup sugar
2 eggs

2 teaspoons baking powder
1 teaspoon baking soda
¼ teaspoon salt
1½ teaspoons vanilla extract
1½ cups flour
¾ cup buttermilk

1. Preheat oven to 350 degrees.
2. In a heavy 10½ inch iron skillet, melt 1 stick of butter. Add brown sugar and heat, stirring constantly, until sugar is dissolved.
3. Remove from heat and arrange 8 pineapple slices, in one layer, in bottom of skillet. Place a cherry in the center of each slice and sprinkle with chopped pecans. Set aside.
4. In a separate mixing bowl, cream 1 stick butter and white sugar. Add eggs and vanilla and mix well.
5. Add powder, soda, salt, and half of flour. Mix until well blended.
6. Add half of buttermilk and mix well again.
7. Add remaining flour, followed by remaining buttermilk, beating well after each addition. Mix batter until smooth.
8. Carefully pour batter into skillet over pineapple slices. Bake 25 to 30 minutes, until knife inserted in center comes out clean.
9. Allow to cool 5 minutes in pan before inverting on serving dish.

Note: If you don't have a large iron skillet, melt the butter and sugar in a separate saucepan and pour into a similarly sized cake pan. Arrange fruit slices and proceed with recipe as described above.

Evening
shadows

Quiet Suppers at Home

Simple Supper 'Neath the Harvest Moon
a quick, filling supper for 4 to 6 hungry workers

Whoso findeth a wife findeth a good thing.—Proverbs 18:22

Summer fades into Indian summer, and those last days of late light find you busy cutting and storing the hay that will feed your cattle through the long months of winter snow. For this yearly ritual, you forgo household chores and spend long hours driving swathers and balers through the vivid green windrows. On towards dusk, he'll stay to stack those last few rows while you drive down to the house and start supper. He arrives tired and hungry, stretching his weary shoulders. Though you both try to pass the last of the evening together, not too long after the dishes are stacked in the sink, you're dozing off in the easy chair, knowing tomorrow will be another long day of carrying and stacking.

Hearty work makes big appetites. For these long days, build a repertoire of quick, stick-to-the-ribs recipes with soothing rich flavor.

Rubbed with a mildly peppery paste and quickly broiled, this simple GRILLED SIRLOIN showcases top-quality lean beef. Sirloins and top rounds take little more effort than clever seasoning and 10 minutes in a hot oven or over your backyard grill.

A creamy celebration of harvest, HAY AND STRAW—an Italian classic—mixes a farmland palette of subtle yellow pasta and alfalfa-green spinach noodles. With leftover ham, tender frozen peas, and piquant Parmesan cheese, this traditional pasta starter plus a crisp green salad, makes a wonderful lunch or a crowd-pleasing supper side.

PANFRIED TOMATOES are a winner all through the harvest season with firm-fleshed fruits of any color. I've added flavorful bread crumbs instead of the expected cornmeal coating for a quick and easy skillet vegetable.

Topped with moist bars of APPLESAUCE CARAMEL CAKE, you've got a special, tasty meal that's easy on the cook, simple enough for little pards to lend a hand, and ready to satisfy a hungry haying crew.

Grilled Sirloin

½ cup brown sugar
1 tablespoon dried lemon peel
1 teaspoon cilantro flakes
½ teaspoon cayenne pepper
¼ teaspoon black pepper

½ teaspoon salt
5 tablespoons olive oil
1 tablespoon red wine
1 sirloin steak approximately 1½–2
    pounds

1. Preheat oven to broil or make a fire under the grill.
2. Combine all of the ingredients, except for the steak, into a thick paste.
3. Rub seasoning mix into both sides of the steak.
4. Broil or grill steak 5 to 6 minutes on a side for medium rare, or longer according to your taste.

Garlic Bread

½ cup butter, softened
2 cloves garlic, minced
½ cup Parmesan cheese
⅛ teaspoon pepper

¼ teaspoon salt
2 teaspoons parsley flakes
1 loaf French or Italian bread, unsliced

1. Preheat oven to 375 degrees.
2. Cream together ingredients for garlic butter. Mix until a smooth paste is formed.
3. Cut bread in half lengthwise; spread each half with garlic butter.
4. Toast on cookie sheet for 8 to 12 minutes, until butter is melted and loaf is barely crunchy.

Hay and Straw

1 stick (8 tablespoons) butter
½ onion chopped fine
1 10-ounce package frozen peas
½ pound ham, chopped
1½ cups heavy cream

1 teaspoon salt
1½ teaspoons black pepper
½ to ¾ cup Parmesan cheese (to taste)
½ pound spinach fettucine noodles
½ pound fettucine noodles

1. Put a large pot of water on to boil.
2. To make the cream sauce, in a large skillet melt ½ stick of butter and sauté onions over medium heat until transparent.
3. Turn heat to high and add frozen peas. Cook 3 minutes, stirring often.
4. Add ham and cook, stirring, about 2 minutes, until warmed through and edges start to crisp.
5. Add 1 cup of cream to skillet and cook until thickened, season to taste with salt and pepper. Set aside.
6. When water boils, cook each pasta as described on package. The spinach pasta may take less time than the regular.
7. When pasta is just tender, drain in sink.
8. In the stock pot, melt ½ stick of butter; stir in ½ cup of cream. When just mixed, add drained pasta and toss over medium heat.
9. Add the cream sauce and Parmesan cheese, re-season with salt and pepper if needed, toss until well coated, and serve.

Panfried Tomatoes

8 firm Roma tomatoes or 4 large
   tomatoes, sliced thick
½ cup seasoned bread crumbs
¼ cup Parmesan cheese
3 saltine crackers, crushed
½ teaspoon salt
⅛ teaspoon pepper

1 teaspoon dried basil leaves
Dash of cayenne
¼ cup milk
Dash of Tabasco sauce
2 tablespoons olive oil
2 tablespoons vegetable oil

1. Combine bread crumbs, crackers, Parmesan, basil, salt, and pepper.
2. Mix the tabasco sauce with milk. Quickly dip the tomato slices in milk, then roll in the bread-crumb mixture on both sides.
3. Heat olive and vegetable oil in skillet.
4. When the oil is sizzling hot, add tomato slices cook about 1 minute on each side, until golden brown.

Applesauce Caramel Cake

1 stick (8 tablespoons) butter or
   margarine
⅔ cup brown sugar
½ cup sugar
3 eggs
2 cups flour
3 teaspoons baking powder
½ cup milk
1 cup applesauce
1 teaspoon cinnamon

¼ teaspoon ground cloves
1 18-ounce package caramel apple dip or
   18 ounces of caramels, melted

Glaze
½ cup confectioner's sugar
½ teaspoon cinnamon
2–4 tablespoons hot water, enough to
   form glaze

1. Preheat oven to 350 degrees. Butter or spray a 9 x 13 baking pan.
2. In a large mixing bowl, cream butter and sugars until thick.
3. Add eggs and mix until well blended.
4. Add flour and baking powder alternately with the milk and apple sauce, and mix until smooth. Add spices and mix well.
5. Pour batter into greased pan.
6. Soften the caramel by resting the bowl in hot water. Drizzle the soft caramel over the cake and, with a lightly oiled knife, marble into the batter.
7. Bake for 25 to 30 minutes, until a knife inserted in center comes out clean. Caution: don't mistake the caramel for underdone cake.
8. Mix the ingredients for the glaze until smooth, and pour over cake immediately upon removing from the oven.
9. Allow to cool slightly in pan and cut into squares.

He Loves Me, He Loves Me Not
a spring supper for 4 to 6

*The hardest task of a girl's life is to prove to a man that his
intentions are serious. —Helen Rowland*

Reach over and take a daisy from your springtime bouquet. Count the soft petals—"He loves me…He loves me…."

In early spring, when lovely wildflowers speckle the green meadows and hillsides, gather a brightly colored bouquet of dazzling forget-me-nots. Resting in a Mason jar on your supper table or tied in bunches drying from the rafters, bright flowers speak an ancient language of love.

Starring in your early spring supper is a thick, choice cut of steak stuffed with vibrant green spinach—one of the season's earliest garden vegetables. Ask your butcher to fashion a deep pocket in the meat, or carefully make the cut yourself. Though this dish is wonderful with any tender, quick-cooking beef steak (sirloin is particularly good), I've chosen top round because the pattern of marbling helps to keep the filling inside the meat. Lightly brushed with butter and seasonings, stuffed steak is an easy-to-prepare elegant entrée that celebrates

spring but is still hearty enough to ward off March's lions.

Beside the steak, offer tender wedges of OVEN POTATOES covered in a delicate chicken broth, a flavorful home-style dish. If you are serving roasted meats (turkey, goose, chicken), use a bit of the pan drippings instead of the bacon for equally delicious results.

HONEY WHEAT BREAD, an unusual batter loaf, has a slightly sweet flavor, a fine crumb, and an unusual nutty texture. This one-bowl loaf that mimics a whole-grain wheat bread is perfect when time is short.

TANGY LEMON CHESS PIE is a variation of a centuries-old American tradition. Ever so slightly tart and sunshine yellow, this lemon-custard dessert is the perfect way to welcome the spring. It is filling without being heavy, sweet without being sugary.

Gathering petals from the table, you know you don't need to wonder.

Spinach-Stuffed Steak

For the Stuffing

1 10½-ounce package frozen spinach
½ medium onion, chopped fine
5 mushrooms, sliced (optional)
2 tablespoons olive oil
3 scallions, chopped
½ cup Parmesan cheese
1 cup cooked rice
1 teaspoon dill
1 tablespoon parsley flakes
¼ teaspoon salt
¼ teaspoon pepper

½ teaspoon nutmeg
1 egg

For the Steak

1 round steak (approximately 2 pounds)
   with a pocket cut
2 tablespoons butter, melted
1 teaspoon lemon juice
½ teaspoon worcestershire sauce
Dash of salt
Dash of pepper
Dash of Tabasco sauce

1. Cook spinach according to package directions; drain.
2. Preheat oven to 400 degrees.
3. In a small skillet, sauté onions and mushrooms in olive oil until tender.
4. Combine with spinach and remaining ingredients for stuffing, set aside.
5. Wash steak and pat dry.
6. Stuff pocket with spinach mixture, working carefully so as not to tear the meat.
7. Secure opening with toothpicks or kitchen thread.
8. Combine butter, lemon juice, salt, pepper, worcestershire, and Tabasco. Carefully brush both sides of the steak with butter mixture and place meat on broiler pan.
9. Cook 8 minutes without turning, then turn oven to broil and cook 4 minutes more. Turn steak, carefully so as not to spill stuffing, baste with remaining butter sauce and broil 5 minutes.
10. Serve sliced across the grain so each piece has piping hot spinach stuffing surrounded by medium-rare meat.

Okra Succotash

4 strips bacon, cut in pieces
1 medium onion, chopped
1 16-ounce bag frozen okra
1 4-ounce can whole green chiles, coarsely chopped

1 16-ounce can sweet corn kernels
½ teaspoon salt
½ teaspoon pepper
¼ teaspoon ground thyme

1. In a large, heavy-bottomed pan over medium heat, sauté bacon and onion together until onion is soft.
2. Add remaining ingredients, cover, turn heat to low and simmer for 25 to 30 minutes, until vegetables are warm and okra is cooked through.

Oven Potato Wedges

6 medium potatoes
Salt and pepper to taste

6 slices bacon
4 cups chicken broth

1. Preheat oven to 350 degrees.
2. Peel potatoes and cut into wedges (about 8 per potato). Place in ovenproof bowl or casserole dish. Sprinkle with salt and pepper.
3. Cut bacon into approximately 1-inch squares and fry over medium-low heat until just starting to crisp. Add bacon and grease to potatoes and toss well.
4. Cover with chicken broth and bake for 1 hour and 15 minutes to 1½ hours, until potatoes are tender but not mushy.

Honey Wheat Bread

½ cup honey
2 eggs, beaten
¾ cup buttermilk, room temperature
¼ teaspoon salt
1 tablespoon baking powder

1 teaspoon baking soda
2 cups flour
1 cup regular Cream of Wheat Cereal
(not instant)

1. Preheat oven to 350 degrees. Oil or spray a large loaf pan.
2. Combine honey, buttermilk, and eggs together in a large mixing bowl.
3. Add salt, powder, and soda and mix well.
4. Beat in flour and cereal until a thick, sticky dough forms.
5. Pour dough into well-greased large loaf pan, and bake for 35 to 40 minutes, until a chewy, golden crust forms.

Lemon Chess Pie

Single Pie Crust (see recipe below)
4 eggs, beaten
2 cups sugar
1½ tablespoons cornmeal

2 tablespoons flour
4 tablespoons butter, melted
½ cup lemon juice
1½ tablespoons lemon peel

1. Preheat oven to 375 degrees.
2. Cream eggs, sugar and melted butter. Add remaining ingredients, and beat well.
3. Carefully pour batter into prepared pie crust. Bake for 40 minutes, until top is golden brown. If top becomes too brown during baking, lightly tent with tin foil. Chill before serving.

Single Pie Crust

1½ cups flour
5 tablespoons butter-flavor vegetable
    shortening
3 tablespoons butter

Dash salt
1 tablespoon lemon juice
4–5 tablespoons ice-cold water

1. Cut shortening into flour until mixture starts to resemble meal.
2. Cut in cold butter until mixture forms a coarse meal.
3. Add lemon juice and just enough water to hold dough together.
4. Wrap and chill for 30 minutes. Roll dough on a lightly floured surface or between 2 sheets of waxed paper to form a circle 2 inches bigger than pie pan.
5. Lay into pie pan. Trim or fold dough to ½ inch of side, and flute edges by pinching dough between thumb and finger of your other hand.
6. With a fork, prick a series of small holes in the bottom of crust.
7. Fill and bake according to Lemon Chess Pie recipe.

Ward off a Winter's Chill
a spicy supper for 4

*Like the best romances, the best meals are warm and sweet,
with enough spice to keep 'em interesting*

Cold winds have loosened summer's tight hold on the country, and suddenly green grasses turn to brown. The morning starts not with a casual ride through the yards to check on new calves but with hurried drives to distant water holes, breaking ice and freeing frozen windmills. Savory dishes simmering on the stove make even bleak days like these glisten with nature's romance.

This rich, piquant CHILI INCA CHUCK ROAST found its inspiration in the native tribes of Mexico and South America who combined chiles and cocoa to tenderize meats and flavor rich, long-cooking stews. Don't be shy about the seemingly exotic mix of ingredients; these flavors blend perfectly and the aroma fills the whole house with the fragrance of homemade specialties spiced with love. The deep red gravy is irresistible ladled over the FRUITED RICE.

Though intended as an easy way to make use of leftover sweet potatoes, you'll find yourself baking extra for more of these light, orange SWEET POTATO CORNCAKES. Try the same recipe with any winter squash.

Though today thought of as a "new" salad green, bitter arugula was a pioneer favorite. Toss a few leaves with lemon juice, olive oil, salt, and pepper for a simple salad with frontier history.

Dessert will be your sweetest triumph. Buttermilk pies were first created as treats when winter made fresh fruit scarce. Today the smooth custard is a visit to a time long past, before the advent of iceboxes and supermarkets.

Look out at the ice-covered pastures and plains, and tackle the evening's chores. Roll up your sleeves. You wash, let him dry. The evening seems especially warm.

Chili Inca Chuck Roast

Olive oil
2–3 cloves of garlic, peeled and sliced
1–1½ pounds chuck roast, about 2 inches
   thick
2 tablespoons of flour, mixed with:
   ¼ teaspoon black pepper
   ¼ teaspoon red pepper
   ¼ teaspoon white pepper
Salt to taste

1 28-ounce can crushed tomatoes
½ cup water
2 cinnamon sticks
1 teaspoon cinnamon
3 teaspoons cocoa
½ teaspoon chili powder
1 teaspoon crushed red pepper flakes
1 7-ounce can whole green chiles
½ cup brown sugar

1. Coat bottom of heavy covered pan with olive oil, add garlic, and place over medium-high heat until garlic begins to fry.
2. Quickly brown roast on all sides, and remove roast from pot.
3. Add all remaining ingredients to pot, stir well, and bring to slow boil.
4. Return roast to pot and return sauce to boil. Cover and reduce heat to very low. Simmer for 3 to 4 hours, until roast is fork tender.

Easy Black-Bean Dip

Remaining Chili Inca Chuck Roast sauce
1 16-ounce can black beans, rinsed and
   drained
1 teaspoon cumin

1½ teaspoons dried cilantro
2 teaspoons lemon juice
1 spring onion, chopped, for garnish

1. Add can of black beans, cumin, and cilantro to the remaining sauce.
2. Simmer for 20 to 30 minutes, until sauce is cooked down.
3. When the beans have cooled, add lemon juice.
4. Purée in the blender. Top with spring onion and serve with tortilla chips.

Fruited Rice

2 cups water
1 cup rice
2 tablespoons butter
¼ teaspoon orange peel
1 11-ounce can mandarin oranges,
    drained, reserving two tablespoons
    syrup

¼ cup raisins (optional)
Salt to taste
Green of one spring onion, chopped
2–3 tablespoons sour cream
¼ cup shredded cheddar cheese

1. Bring water and reserved syrup to boil in saucepan.
2. Add rice, butter, and orange peel. Cover and reduce heat to low. Cook for 20 minutes, or until liquid has evaporated. Rice will be quite moist.
3. Over low heat, stir in drained oranges and raisins; heat through.
4. To serve, sprinkle with cheddar cheese, top with spicy sauce from the chuck roast, a dollop of sour cream and chopped green onion. Don't skimp on the toppings, it is the mix of flavors in this dinner that make the meal really special.

Note: Use leftover rice from this recipe in *Festive Rice Pudding,* recipe page 69.

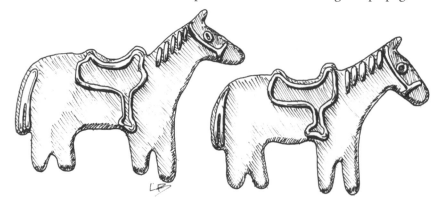

Sweet Potato Corncakes

Makes 8 jumbo or about 16 small biscuits

1 cup yellow cornmeal
1¼ cups flour
1 teaspoon salt
1 tablespoon baking powder

3 tablespoons orange marmalade
1 cup cooked, mashed sweet potatoes
2 tablespoons butter, melted
1 cup buttermilk

1. Preheat oven to 400. Oil or spray cookie sheet.
2. In a medium-sized mixing bowl, combine dry ingredients.
3. In a smaller bowl, mix marmalade into sweet potatoes.
4. Add butter, half of sweet potato mixture, and half of buttermilk to dry ingredients, stirring well. Repeat.
5. Drop by heaping spoonfuls onto a greased cookie sheet, leaving about 2 inches between biscuits.
6. Bake for 15 to 20 minutes, until cooked through.

Lone-Star Buttermilk Custard Pie

Despite the good dry mixes on the market, for this pie I insist on cool, fresh buttermilk from the churn or from the dairy case.

One Graham Cracker Crust recipe
   (opposite page)
3 eggs, well beaten
1½ cups sugar
3 tablespoons flour

½ cup butter (1 stick), melted
1 cup buttermilk
¼ teaspoon nutmeg plus a dash for the top
1 teaspoon of scotch whiskey or vanilla
   extract

1. Preheat oven to 350 degrees.
2. In a medium-size mixing bowl, add sugar and flour to beaten eggs and whisk.
3. Pour in melted butter and buttermilk, then mix. Add nutmeg and whiskey or vanilla extract. Combine thoroughly.
4. Pour filling into pre-baked graham cracker crust; top with dash of nutmeg.
5. Bake for 30 to 40 minutes, until a knife inserted about 1½ inches from the side comes out clean.

Note: While baking, you may want to lightly cover the edges of the crust with tin foil so they don't become too brown or crisp.

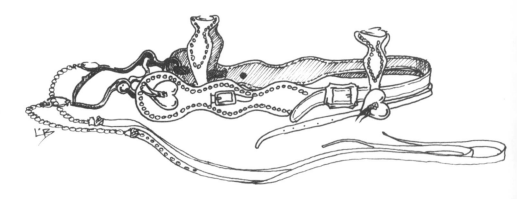

Graham Cracker Crust

1¼–1½ cups graham cracker crumbs
   (10 to 14 crackers)
6 tablespoons butter, melted

2 tablespoons sugar
¼ teaspoon nutmeg
1 egg beaten with 2 tablespoons water

1. Preheat oven to 350 degrees.
2. Place all ingredients in a bowl and mix until crumbs are moistened.
3. Pat mixture into the bottom and up the sides of an 8- or 9-inch pie pan.
4. Bake for 3 to 4 minutes.
5. Brush crust with a thin coating of egg and water mixture. This will seal the crust. If you prefer a soft-bottomed pie, omit this step.
6. Return to oven and bake for 3 to 4 minutes more.
7. Fill, then bake according to Lone-Star Buttermilk Pie recipe. Allow to cool slightly.

VARIATION: Instead of brushing the crust with egg and water glaze, first bake the crust for the full 6 to 8 minutes, then thinly coat with your choice of peach or apricot jam or orange marmalade mixed with a bit of water. Make certain the portions of the crust that will hold the liquid are well covered.

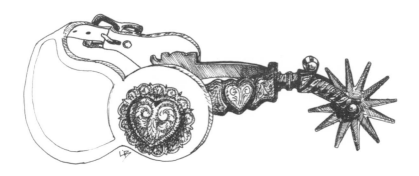

Home Fires
a homey menu for 4

If you want to be loved, be lovable. —Ovid

Two pairs of boots are drying by the stove. Comfortably resting in the old plaid easy chair, he is carefully braiding thin lengths of rawhide into a handsome new quirt. Barely an arm's length away, peacefully keeping time in a weathered wooden rocker, you're finishing up the last cables on your grandson's navy blue sweater. Now and again you glance his way and smile, or amble off to check on dinner. He watches as you walk from the room.

In the oven are dishes he remembers from when your marriage was young. He was drawing a cowhand's short pay; towards the end of the month money was tight. Some days were steak, and others have been meatloaf, but looking back you wouldn't trade even one.

Spiced with zesty sausage, FINALLY GREAT MEATLOAF benefits from the sharp tang of Parmesan cheese and disappears quickly.

If homemade bread sounds like too much work after a busy day of riding and roping, CRUSTY GARLIC ROLLS are the answer. They mix up in minutes and are quickly shaped into luscious, thick, chewy breads.

Our foremothers rose long before sunrise and mixed yeast sponges into a family's supply of light breads. Lucky children awoke to kitchens heavily perfumed with warm bowls of proofing dough. Those skillful kitchen matrons might have frowned at my fondness for quick biscuits and batter loaves, yet these easy breads turn everyday dinners into events…and leave the cook time to join in the fun.

FESTIVE RICE PUDDING, inspired by Mexico's terrific custard creations, is an effortless dessert and a great way to use up leftover apples, pears, or canned fruits.

"Seems like old times," he smiles.

Finally Great Meatloaf

1 pound Italian sausage (sweet or hot)
1 pound ground beef
2 eggs, beaten
1 teaspoon pepper
1½ teaspoons salt
½ cup seasoned Italian bread crumbs

½ cup Parmesan cheese
3 tablespoons parsley flakes
1 medium onion, chopped
3–4 cloves garlic, chopped
¼ pound mozzarella cheese, cut into
    ¼- inch thick slices

1. Preheat oven to 375 degrees.
2. In a large bowl, knead together all the ingredients (except mozzarella).
3. Place half of the meat mixture in a large loaf pan, cover with cheese, and top
   with remaining meat. Be sure the cheese is fully encased by the meat.
4. Bake for 1 hour and 15 minutes to 1½ hours. Serve with chunky tomato sauce.

Chunky Tomato Sauce

3 tablespoons olive oil
½ medium onion, chopped
2 cloves garlic, chopped
1 28-ounce can whole tomatoes, drained
    and chopped
1 28-ounce can crushed tomatoes

½ teaspoon cinnamon
½ teaspoon sugar
1 teaspoon oregano
2 tablespoons parsley flakes
1–2 inner stalks of celery with leaves
1½ tablespoons butter

1. In a medium saucepan, sauté onions and garlic in olive oil until soft.
2. Add remaining ingredients, except for butter, and bring to a boil.
3. Lower heat and allow to bubble for 1½ hours. Stir in butter, then cook
   5 minutes more. Serve over hot meatloaf and noodles.

Buttered Pasta

1 pound rigatoni noodles
2 tablespoons butter
½ cup Parmesan cheese

1½ tablespoons parsley flakes
Salt and pepper to taste

1. Cook noodles according to package directions, and drain.
2. Return to cooking pot over a very low flame and stir in butter.
3. When butter has melted, add remaining ingredients; toss until well mixed.

Crusty Garlic Rolls

3 tablespoons olive oil
6 cloves garlic, finely chopped
1 medium onion, finely chopped
3½ cups flour
1 teaspoon salt

1 tablespoon baking powder
2 tablespoons parsley flakes
1 can warm beer
1 egg, beaten
4 tablespoons butter, melted

1. Preheat oven to 350 degrees. Butter or spray a 9- to 10-inch pan or skillet.
2. Sauté onion and garlic in olive oil until soft and slightly browned; set aside.
3. Combine flour, salt, powder, and parsley. Beat egg and beer together and add all at once to flour mixture; stir until just mixed.
4. On a lightly floured surface, gently knead sautéed onion and garlic into the dough.
5. Roll the dough into 18 to 20 balls, dip into melted butter, and arrange in pan so they are just touching.
6. Bake 35 to 40 minutes, until golden brown on top.

Note: If desired, make larger rolls for terrific sandwiches and hamburger buns.

Festive Rice Pudding

3 eggs
1 cup sugar
1 cup milk
1 cup cream
½ teaspoon mace

2 cups cooked rice
1 11-ounce can mandarin oranges,
    drained
Nutmeg for dusting

1. Preheat oven to 325 degrees.
2. In a large ovenproof bowl or casserole dish, beat together eggs and sugar until thick.
3. Add milk, cream, and mace, and mix until well blended.
4. Fold in rice and oranges. Dust top with nutmeg.
5. Bake for 45 minutes. Serve warm or cold.

Thinking of You
a soothing supper for 4

Absence sharpens love, presence strengthens it. —*Thomas Fuller*

Chasing the gold buckle keeps him away most of the rodeo season. Thinking of you and your cozy home, he misses the steady music of the rusty screen drumming against the bedroom window (hadn't he promised to fix that?), the merry creak of barn doors, the distantly familiar taste of your home cooking. Simple things are so powerful in memory. He drives on down the road, wishing he could be with you all the time.

He's drawn a good horse at the show just 300 miles away. It's the closest he's been in weeks. He'll be home for just a few days before he's up again in Cheyenne. You're fixing a special dinner to soothe his road-weary soul.

Cooking fruit and meats together has passed in and out of fashion for centuries. Although it might be an unusual dish in your kitchen, this combination of mild, white pork and sweet pears is hard to beat. Bubbling slowly in a faithful iron pot, PORK AND PEAR STEW is the kind of recipe that becomes a treasured heirloom. Newlywed brides call for instructions; travelers request the simple dish as a welcome-home supper.

Another reassuring favorite, ACORN SQUASH CUSTARD is sweetened by delicate maple syrup. Served in the deep green acorn-squash shells, this side is based on a favorite colonial pumpkin dessert. The sweetness and smooth, mild texture enhance the clove-scented stew.

White or yellow, sugar-sweet or savory hot, each small area of every region has it's own special recipe for quick batter corn breads, just waiting to soak up the last bit of sauce. The cream-style corn and buttermilk combine to make this CREAMY CORN BREAD a rich, smooth, never-dry loaf.

Followed by peppery OLD-FASH-IONED GINGERBREAD, this easy supper is a meal that lives on in memories and calls him back down the gravel road to home.

Pork and Pear Stew

1½–2 pounds pork (shoulder steak, pork sirloin end, picnic roast, butt roast, or rib end), cut into 2-inch pieces

1 29-ounce can of pears with liquid, coarsely chopped

1 onion, chopped

3 carrots, peeled and sliced about ½ inch thick

2 14½-ounce cans chili-style tomatoes (See Note)

½ tomato can of water

2 bay leaves

¼ cup molasses

12 whole cloves

½ teaspoon poultry seasoning

½ teaspoon nutmeg

1 teaspoon cinnamon

1½ teaspoon garlic powder

2 tablespoon worcestershire sauce

Salt and pepper to taste

1. Combine all ingredients in Dutch oven or stock pot. (Include any bones in the pot to season the stew.)
2. Bring to a boil over medium-high heat; reduce heat to low (stew should be quietly bubbling).
3. Cook uncovered for 3 to 4 hours, or until carrots are soft and liquid has cooked down to a thick gravy, stir occasionally, and adjust seasonings to taste.

Note: If your grocery doesn't stock this specialty product, use the same amount of stewed tomatoes seasoned with extra chili powder and a dash of cilantro flakes.

Acorn Squash Custard

*4 small acorn squash that will stand up
   on the stem end*
4 eggs
½ cup maple syrup

⅛ teaspoon nutmeg
⅛ teaspoon cinnamon
¼ teaspoon allspice
2 cups half-and-half

1. Bake squash for 15 minutes at 350 degrees.
2. Beat together eggs and syrup, then add spices and half-and-half and mix well.
   Set aside.
3. Carefully slice the top ½ inch off each squash; reserve tops. Scoop out seeds
   and   string pulp, discard.
4. Fill each prepared squash with custard mixture to ½ inch from the top
   of cavity.
5. Lower oven heat to 325 degrees, and bake squashes, standing upright, for
   40 minutes more, or until custard is firmly set.
6. Replace tops and return to oven for 5 minutes.

Creamy Corn Bread

1½ cups yellow cornmeal
1 cup flour
¼ cup sugar
1½ teaspoons baking powder
½ teaspoon baking soda

½ teaspoon salt
1 cup buttermilk
1 egg, well beaten
1 16-ounce can cream-style corn
4 tablespoons butter, melted

1. Preheat oven to 350 degrees. Butter or spray a 7 x 11 baking pan.
2. In a large mixing bowl, blend dry ingredients.
3. Add buttermilk, beaten egg, and corn. Stir into a thick batter.
4. Mix in melted butter.
5. Pour batter into pan and bake for 30 to 40 minutes, until knife inserted in center comes out clean. Serve hot.

Old-Fashioned Gingerbread

2 cups flour
2 teaspoons baking soda
2 teaspoons ginger
1½ teaspoons cinnamon
½ teaspoon salt
½ teaspoon ground cloves
½ teaspoon nutmeg
½ teaspoon black pepper
1 stick butter, softened

½ cup brown sugar
½ cup white sugar
1 egg
1 cup molasses
1 cup boiling water

For the Glaze
3 tablespoons orange juice
¾ cup confectioners sugar

1. Preheat oven to 350 degrees. Grease a 9-inch square baking pan, large oven-proof skillet, or individual muffin tins with non-stick cooking spray or shortening.
2. Combine dry ingredients in mixing bowl.
3. Cream butter with sugars, add eggs, and mix well. Blend in molasses and water.
4. Add dry ingredients to molasses mixture; mix until blended.
5. Pour into prepared pan and bake for 35 to 45 minutes (15 to 20 minutes for muffins), until knife inserted in center comes out clean.
6. Mix glaze. Pour over hot cake immediately after it comes from the oven.
7. Serve with warm applesauce or whipped cream.

Balcony Scene
an easy evening meal for 4 to 6

*The joys of life are porridge and stew, a donkey to ride,
and a wife to drive it.—Arab proverb*

In *Bend Of The River* Jimmy Stewart guides a wagon train of settlers to the Oregon's rich Columbia River country and finds love on the way. Voluptuous Jane Russell nursed Billy the Kid back to health and became his wife as he lay delirious with fever in 1943's notorious screen fable, *The Outlaw*. Even stalwart John Wayne wasn't immune from love's spell. In John Ford's masterful film *Stagecoach,* beautiful Claire Trevor led "the Duke" headlong into romance.

In classic celluloid westerns, love affairs are revealed not by passionate words or fiery deeds but the shared triumph over seemingly impossible odds. Instead of a weekday meal in the kitchen, stage a silver-screen supper by the bunkhouse VCR. Try this simple-to-prepare menu of bite-sized treats.

TANGY BEEF KABOBS, spiced by a zesty coating of yogurt and lemon, are delicious broiled in the oven or over the backyard grill. The unusual marinade is equally good with lamb, chicken, or pork. The clever mix of seasonings blends perfectly with SCENTED RICE'S fragrant spices, or combined with grilled onions and tomatoes makes a dandy pocket-bread sandwich.

Vividly green and flavorful, the DILLED SPINACH CASSEROLE is wonderful just simply baked, or the same combination of flavors, when topped with a delicate cream sauce, makes an excellent filling for stuffed pasta shells or baked veal breast. On the side, serve a piquant GARBANZO AND FETA SALAD with a tart, garlicky dressing. Not everything, or everyone in life should be mild.

Later in the evening, as Randolph Scott corrals the last outlaw or Gary Cooper hangs up his six-guns, bring out coffee and trays of ROLLED APPLE CAKES. A sweet ending. Girl gets boy. Boy gets dessert.

Tangy Beef Kabobs

1 cup yogurt
½ cup lemon juice
¼ cup olive oil
1 tablespoon parsley flakes
½ teaspoon garlic powder
¼ teaspoon salt
¼ teaspoon turmeric

Dash of mace
Dash of cayenne pepper
1½–2 pounds sirloin or other tender cut,
    trimmed and cut in cubes
4 medium onions, peeled and cut in
    eighths
Barbecue skewers

1. In a large bowl or locking plastic bag, mix all the ingredients, except for the meat and onions.
2. Add meat and allow to marinate in refrigerator 1 hour.
3. Preheat broiler or prepare fire.
4. Thread meat onto skewers alternately with cut onions. If you are using wood skewers, soak them first and be sure to cover entire length with meat and onions so the sticks won't burn under the broiler.
5. Broil or grill 4 to 5 minutes on a side for medium rare, or longer, depending on your preference.

Scented Rice

3 cups chicken stock, or water with 2
    bouillon cubes added
¾ teaspoon dried lemon peel
3 tablespoons butter
¼ teaspoon salt

Dash pepper
¼ teaspoon paprika
¼ teaspoon ground ginger
3 whole cloves
1½ cups raw rice

1. In a saucepan with a tight-fitting lid, combine all ingredients except rice, and bring to a boil over medium-high heat.
2. Add the rice, cover, and reduce heat to low. Simmer for 20 minutes.
3. Serve topped with tangy kabobs.

Dilled Spinach Casserole

2 10-ounce packages frozen chopped
    spinach, thawed and drained
3 eggs, beaten
3 tablespoons cream
1½ tablespoons dried dill weed
4 tablespoons parsley flakes

½ teaspoon garlic powder
½ teaspoon dried lemon peel
½ teaspoon nutmeg
½ teaspoon salt
¼ teaspoon black pepper

1. Preheat oven to 350 degrees. Butter or spray an 8 x 8 baking pan or casserole.
2. Combine all ingredients and mix until well blended.
3. Pour into pan and bake 30 minutes, just until firm.

Garbanzo Feta Salad

1 cucumber, peeled and diced
3 Roma tomatoes or 1 large tomato, diced
½ small red onion, diced
1 15-ounce can garbanzo beans, drained
¼ cup olive oil
¼ cup lemon juice
½ tablespoon red wine vinegar

¼ teaspoon salt
⅛ teaspoon pepper
1 tablespoon parsley flakes
½ teaspoon oregano
¼ teaspoon garlic powder
2 ounces feta (or other very sharp) cheese,
   crumbled

1. Mix all ingredients together. Refrigerate several hours before serving.

Note: For a quick lunch, mix a can of tuna with this tangy salad and serve with warm tortillas or chips.

Rolled Apple Cakes

For the Dough

1½ cups flour

½ cup sugar

¼ teaspoon salt

1 teaspoon baking powder

4 tablespoons cream cheese

1 egg

¼ cup oil

1 teaspoon vanilla

For the Filling

4 tart apples, peeled, cored, and cubed

¾ cup chopped pecans

½ cup raisins

3 tablespoons flour

½ cup brown sugar

¼ cup sugar

½ teaspoon dried lemon peel

1 teaspoon cinnamon

½ teaspoon nutmeg

3 tablespoons butter

2–3 tablespoons milk

3 tablespoons sugar for dusting

1. Combine the flour, sugar, salt, and baking powder for the dough.
2. Mix in cream cheese until mixture begins to look flaky.
3. In a separate bowl, beat together the egg, vanilla and oil. Make a well in the center of flour mixture and pour in liquid. Stir until just mixed.
4. Turn dough onto lightly floured surface, knead until just smooth.
5. Wrap dough in wax paper and refrigerate at least an hour, or overnight.
6. Combine all the filling ingredients, except the butter. Toss well.
7. Preheat oven to 350 degrees.
8. On a floured surface, roll half the dough into a rectangle 14 x 11 inches.
9. Drain excess liquid from filling, and spread half along the long side of the dough, about 4 inches from the edge. Dot with 1 tablespoon butter. Fold uncovered dough over filling and continue to roll, forming a tight log.
11. Carefully place filled roll on a cookie sheet. Brush top with milk and sprinkle lightly with sugar. Repeat with remainder of dough and filling.
12. Bake 40 to 45 minutes, until filling is soft and dough is golden brown. Remove from oven, and while hot, cut rolls into 1½-inch slices.

Home on the Range
supper for 4

A lady's imagination is very rapid; it jumps from admiration to love, from love to matrimony in a moment. —Jane Austen, Pride and Prejudice

Far from city streets, dreamily tucked into a lush green draw is a crisp white cottage. A fireplace glows invitingly through the lengthening evening shadows. It's a home on the range like the fabled cabin school children sing about.

He can't wait to make it back each night. His "home on the range" could be a city apartment or beach-front bungalow. More than just a western cottage, it's a lasting address of the heart.

Inside, warm on the stove, a tasty supper waits for his hard-working hands. Without the endless stirring of traditional gravies, SMOTHERED PORK CHOPS cook down to a savory combination of tender white meat and thick sauce. Accented with soft onions and tart apples, it's a dish made to ward off evening's nippy breezes, a handy one-pan main course.

SOUR-CREAM MASHED POTATOES are a homey, dinnertime delight capped with a generous topping of creamy pork gravy and dusted with black pepper. Soak up that rich sauce with nutty, light brown RYE BISCUITS.

A wonderful dish for finicky eaters who protest meals even slightly more adventurous than meat and potatoes, SWEET AND SOUR CABBAGE BOIL is a lovely purple treat.

After dinner, like the charmed residents of that simple cottage, leave the dishes to soak. Add a piece to the jigsaw puzzle or enjoy a friendly game of cards. Afterwards curl up in an overstuffed arm chair or a soft, cuddly love seat and open a pleasant, ginger-scented PEAR DUMPLING.

Whether sitting by the dancing firelight or looking out together across a downtown balcony, you'll never hear a "discouraging word" when you have welcomed the night with a hearty, homey, evening meal.

Smothered Pork Chops

¾ cup flour
1 teaspoon salt
½ teaspoon pepper
1 teaspoon rubbed sage
½ teaspoon thyme
½ teaspoon garlic

6 pork chops
¼ cup oil
1 tart apple, quartered and sliced
2 large onions, sliced and separated into
   rings
2 cups water

1. Combine flour and spices, dredge pork chops in mixture.
2. In a skillet with a tight-fitting lid, heat oil until hot but not smoking. Add chops and lightly brown on both sides. Remove chops and set aside.
3. Add apple and onions to skillet. Add more oil if necessary.
4. When onions are softened, layer chops in skillet with onions and apples. Add 2 cups of water, cover tightly, and cook over medium-low heat 35 to 45 minutes, until chops are done and gravy has thickened.

Sour-Cream Mashed Potatoes

5–6 large potatoes, cut into 8 pieces
½ teaspoon salt
½ teaspoon black pepper
½ teaspoon garlic powder

4 tablespoons butter
½ cup sour cream
Chopped chives for garnish (optional)

1. In a stock pot, cover cut potatoes with cold water and bring to a boil.
2. Cook for 20 minutes or until tender. Quickly drain potatoes and return to pot.
3. Over very low heat, mash potatoes (with peel) with the back of a spoon or masher, and stir in remaining ingredients (except chives). Serve sprinkled with chives.

Sweet and Sour Cabbage Boil

½ red cabbage, shredded
½ green cabbage, shredded
2 tart apples, quartered and sliced
2 tablespoons butter
½ teaspoon salt

¼ teaspoon pepper
1½ cups water
¼ cup cider vinegar
¾ cup brown sugar
1 tablespoon flour

1. In a sauce pan, combine cabbage, apples, butter, salt, pepper, and water. Bring to a boil and cook for 15 to 20 minutes, or until cabbage is tender.
2. In a small bowl, mix together vinegar, brown sugar, and flour. Pour into boiling cabbage and cook until sauce begins to thicken, about 5 minutes more.

Rye Biscuits

Makes about 16 tender biscuits

2 cups flour
1 cup rye flour
4 teaspoons baking powder
1 teaspoon salt
½ cup vegetable shortening

2 tablespoons natural (unsweetened)
   applesauce
1 egg, beaten
½ cup milk
2 tablespoons butter, melted

1. Combine flours, powder, and salt in a large mixing bowl.
2. Cut in shortening until mixture resembles a coarse meal.
3. Combine applesauce and egg. Add to flour mixture and stir until just blended.
4. Add milk and stir until just mixed. Turn dough out on a lightly floured work surface and knead until well blended.
5. Roll or pat dough out to ½ inch thick, and cut out with biscuit cutter.
6. Place cut biscuits on cookie sheet so they are just barely touching. Brush tops with melted butter and bake for 12 to 15 minutes, until lightly browned.

Pear Dumplings

For the Syrup

1 cup water
½ cup sugar
¼ teaspoon nutmeg
¼ teaspoon cinnamon
2½ tablespoons butter

For the Dough

2 cups flour
¼ cup sugar
¾ cup butter-flavored vegetable shortening
½ cup cold milk

For the Filling

4 pears
4 tablespoons brown sugar
8 small (¼ to ½ inch long) pieces crystallized ginger or ½ teaspoon of ginger mixed with 2 tablespoons white sugar
Dash nutmeg
2 tablespoons sugar for dusting

1. Combine the ingredients for the syrup in a saucepan over medium heat. Stirring constantly, heat until the butter has melted. Set aside.
2. Preheat the oven to 375 degrees.
3. In a large bowl, combine the flour and the sugar for the dough. Cut in the shortening until the mixture resembles coarse meal.
4. Add the milk and knead until dough forms a ball, being careful not to handle the dough too much. Set aside while you prepare the fruit.
5. Core each pear and peel the top half. If desired, leave the bottom ½ inch of the fruit intact so the filling will not leak out.
6. On lightly floured surface, roll out the dough to approximately ⅛ inch thick.
7. Cut the dough in 4 equal pieces and place a pear in the center of each.
8. Fill the cavity of each pear with 1 tablespoon brown sugar and 2 pieces of ginger. Dust the tops with nutmeg. Close dough around pears, pinching to seal.
9. Place pears in a lightly buttered baking dish, pour reserved sauce over top, and dust tops with sugar. Bake 45 minutes, basting 2 or 3 times with syrup.
10. Serve with a spoonful of syrup and a dollop of spiced whipped cream (a little cinnamon or nutmeg is good), topped by a piece of candied ginger.

Red
letter days

Memories to Share

A First Supper for Two

○ ♡ ○ ♡ ○ ♡ ○

Men always want to be a woman's first love—
women like to be a man's last romance.—Oscar Wilde

The table's set with bright red bandanna napkins, the coffee pot is freshly filled. Your heart feels jittery and light, like a wobbly young calf on fresh green grass. Suddenly, the doorbell rings. Your heart is pounding in your chest as you innocently swing open the door and say, "Hi."

A crooked smile, and all at once you're sure everything will be all right. "Just hang your coat anywhere," you casually chime. "C'mon in the kitchen, dinner's nearly ready."

CHICKEN-FRIED STEAK is perhaps the West's regional favorite, found in every cow camp kitchen and coffee shop. It's as hard to improve as it is to ruin and makes a welcome supper for any visiting cowhand. Fry your steaks as the cheesy GREEN-CHILI GRITS finish baking, then keep both dishes warm in the oven as you confidently stir up thick, white CREAM GRAVY.

For no reason at all, I worry every time I make gravy. Though I always use these same measurements, and have never had a gravy fail, each time as I'm adding liquid—I may look cool and calm on the outside—I'm staring hopefully into the saucepan until that happy moment when thin liquid suddenly turns thick.

Quickly fill a homey crock with your cream gravy and set everything, including a chilled pitcher of lemony iced tea ("house wine of the West"), on the table.

So far, so good. He's casually impressed by your graceful style. But you've still got an ace up your sleeve. Tall, dark, and sinfully chocolate, I've heard this dessert pronounced "too good for kids." For parties, my mother would frost this deep-flavored cake with fresh whipped cream, but decadent COFFEE BUTTERCREAM FROSTING is deliciously adult, a sugar-sweet knockout punch.

Linger just a minute at the door and send him along with a chocolate package to go, a foil-wrapped reminder of a sweet evening passed together.

Chicken-Fried Steak

*2 cube beef steaks, or one round
   steak, cut into serving-size pieces
   (¾ to 1 pound total weight)*
½ cup flour
¼ teaspoon paprika
¼ teaspoon garlic powder
¼ teaspoon salt

⅛ teaspoon black pepper
⅛ teaspoon chili powder
1 egg, beaten
1 tablespoon milk
Dash Tabasco
Oil for frying

1. If you are using round steak, cut visible fat from the meat and tenderize steaks with kitchen mallet. (This step is not necessary with cube steaks.)
2. Mix flour and spices in small bowl. In a separate bowl, combine egg, milk, and Tabasco.
3. Heat oil (¼ inch deep) in skillet until a drop of water causes the oil to sizzle and bubble.
4. Dip steaks in flour mixture, then in egg, and then in flour mixture again.
5. Lay steaks in hot oil and fry until lightly browned on one side. Turn and fry until browned and meat is cooked through. Fry in batches if necessary (keeping the cooked meat warm in a 200-degree oven). Don't crowd the pan.

Cream Gravy

3 tablespoons butter or pan drippings
3 tablespoons flour

2 cups half-and-half
Salt and pepper to taste

1. Melt butter in saucepan, add flour, and stir with fork or whisk until smooth.
2. Over medium heat, gradually add half-and-half, stirring constantly until gravy thickens.
3. Season with salt and plenty of strong, black pepper.

Green-Chili Grits

2 tablespoons butter
1 medium onion, chopped
2 cups water
½ cup grits
½ cup cheddar cheese, shredded
½ teaspoon garlic powder
¼ teaspoon salt

¼ teaspoon pepper
⅛ teaspoon chili powder
1 tablespoon parsley flakes
1 teaspoon cilantro flakes
2 eggs, beaten
2 whole roasted green chiles (canned is fine), seeded, and coarsely chopped

1. Preheat oven to 350 degrees. Butter or spray a casserole.
2. Sauté onions in butter until translucent.
3. In another saucepan, boil water, stir in grits, and cook—stirring occasionally—for 30 minutes. (For instant grits, follow package directions).
4. When grits are thick and have a creamy texture, add sautéed onions and remaining ingredients. Stir until well mixed.
5. Pour mixture into a casserole and bake for 80 minutes.

Tomato Corn Salad

1 15½ -ounce can sweet corn
4 Roma tomatoes (or 1½ larger variety), seeded and chopped
½ green pepper, seeded and chopped
½ medium red onion, chopped

½ teaspoon basil flakes
¼ cup olive oil
¼ cup lemon juice
Salt and pepper to taste

1. Combine vegetables and basil in serving bowl.
2. In a separate bowl, mix together olive oil and lemon juice, pour over vegetables. Add salt and pepper and toss well.
3. Refrigerate at least 30 minutes before serving.

Grandma Mary's Chocolate Cake

1 recipe Coffee Buttercream Frosting
  (See recipe below)
2 cups flour
⅔ cup cocoa
1 teaspoon baking powder
2 teaspoons baking soda
2 teaspoons cinnamon
½ cup butter

1 cup white sugar
1 cup brown sugar
2 eggs, beaten
2 teaspoons vanilla
3 tablespoons plus 1 teaspoon vegetable oil
½ cup hot coffee
1 cup buttermilk or sour milk

1. Preheat oven to 350 degrees. Grease and flour two 9-inch round baking pans.
2. In a mixing bowl, combine flour, cocoa, powder, soda, and cinnamon.
3. In large bowl, cream together butter and sugars, add eggs, and beat well.
4. Add oil and coffee and mix until blended.
5. Add ½ of dry ingredients, mix, and add ½ cup of buttermilk. Mix well. Repeat.
6. Pour batter into two greased and floured 9-inch round baking pans.
7. Bake for 25 to 30 minutes, until knife inserted in center comes out clean.
   Let rest in pans 10 to 15 minutes before removing to wire racks to cool. Frost.

Coffee Buttercream Frosting

2 eggs yolks
4 tablespoons butter
3 cups confectioners (powdered) sugar

1 tablespoon vanilla
1 tablespoon cocoa
4–6 tablespoons hot coffee

1. Cream eggs yolks and butter.
2. Add sugar, vanilla, cocoa, and four tablespoons of the coffee, and mix well.
3. If needed, add more coffee to make a smooth, spreadable frosting.

Impressing the In-Laws
a tasty meal for 4 to 6 important guests

*Nothing is more sure to keep a man a life-long bachelor
than searching for the perfect woman.*

Honey, you're just worrying over nothing," he says while putting out the glasses. "They're gonna love you just as much as I do."

There are few situations more nerve-racking, more fraught with potential disaster than a first dinner with future in-laws. Even the most charming couple, seen across a potential daughter-in-law's table, can appear to judge each step, seemingly searching for the smallest slip.

Such times call for fail-safe recipes, served with careless grace and at least an outer air of warm confidence. You'll win their hearts with this simple collection of make-ahead masterpieces and your charming conversation.

Laced with tangy flavor, GREEN-CHILI CHICKEN ROLLBACKS are easily prepared dinner bundles accented by the mellow surprise of cheddar cheese. Marinate and assemble the chicken dish early in the afternoon (store tightly

covered in the refrigerator), if you'd like. Before baking, generously baste the chicken with the marinade, reserving some for the easy cream sauce.

Creamy and familiar SCALLOPED POTATOES are an easy side dish. While the mixture bakes down to a hearty, buttery sauce, you'll have plenty of time to set the table, feed the horses, or give the kitchen one last sweep.

As she reaches for her second flaky ONION ROLL, his mother will be wondering where you ever get the time. He squeezes your hand under the table.

Smile through the sound of forks scraping dessert plates for one last bite of BUTTERMILK POUND CAKE drenched in COCONUT DESSERT SALSA while your future mother-in-law shares her guarded secret for airy cakes.

"Welcome to the family," he laughs warmly. Phew!

Scalloped Potatoes

¼ cup flour
¼ teaspoon onion powder
Dash paprika
6 medium potatoes

3 tablespoons butter
1 cup cream
Salt and pepper to taste
2½ cups milk

1. Preheat oven to 350 degrees. Coat Dutch oven with non-stick cooking spray.
2. Combine flour and spices in large bowl or locking plastic bag.
3. Peel (if desired) and slice potatoes into approximately ¼-inch-thick rounds. Dust with flour, either by tossing in bowl or shaking in bag of mixture.
4. Arrange ⅓ of potato slices in a lightly buttered Dutch oven, dot row with 1 tablespoon of butter cut into 6 to 8 pieces, and sprinkle with salt and pepper. Repeat with remainder of potato slices.
5. Combine milk and cream and pour over potatoes.
6. Bake for 1½ hours or until sauce thickens nicely.

VARIATION: For a change of pace, try ½ cup of grated cheese on top (add the cheese after the potatoes have baked for an hour) or layer crumbled bacon or chopped ham on top of the potatoes.

Green-Chili Chicken Rollbacks

Marinade
½ cup olive oil
¼ cup lemon juice
¼ cup lime juice
½ large onion, chopped
½ teaspoon garlic powder
¼ teaspoon nutmeg
½ teaspoon cumin
½ teaspoon chili powder
1 teaspoon cilantro flakes

For the Chicken Bundles
4–6 chicken breasts, boned
1 small can whole roasted green chiles
4–6 ½-ounce chunks cheddar cheese

Bread Crumb Mixture
¾ cup bread crumbs
1 tablespoon parsley flakes
¼ teaspoon garlic powder
1 tablespoon Parmesan

For the Cream Sauce
Reserved marinade
1 tablespoon flour
1 tablespoon butter
1 cup half-and-half
¼ cup tequila (optional)

Toothpicks, kitchen twine, or the green from spring onions to tie the chicken bundles

Continued on next page

Green Chili Chicken Rollbacks

1. Mix all the ingredients for the marinade and set aside.
2. Butterfly each breast so the meat is laid out flat.
3. With a kitchen mallet or the handle of a heavy knife, pound each butterflied breast lightly until meat is approximately ½ inch thick.
4. Place chicken in marinade for 15 to 20 minutes.
5. Preheat oven to 350 degrees.
6. Remove chicken from marinade and lay out flat on the counter. Reserve leftover marinade.
7. Top each chicken filet with ½ (cut lengthwise) green chili and a cube of cheddar cheese.
8. Roll the chicken and chile around the cheese, using the skin to wrap the bundle. If necessary to keep the melted cheese inside the baked roll, tie with kitchen twine or secure the opening with toothpicks.
9. Combine all the ingredients for the bread-crumb mixture.
10. Coat each bundle with bread-crumb mixture and place in baking dish.
11. Bake for 25 to 35 minutes, until crumb topping is golden brown and chicken is cooked through.

For the Sauce
1. Pour remaining marinade with the chopped onions into a medium saucepan.
2. Add butter and cook over medium-high heat until onions are softened.
3. Stir in flour and cook until a thick paste forms and flour is cooked.
4. Add-half-and half in a thin stream, stirring constantly.
5. When sauce has thickened, stir in tequila, cook a few moments more stirring well, and serve immediately alongside baked chicken bundles.

Note: This tangy dish is easily doubled or even tripled to feed a crowd. But make plenty. It really is good!

Company Green Beans

1 pound fresh, or 1 package frozen green
  beans
4 tablespoons butter
6 mushrooms, sliced

¼ medium onion, minced
1 clove garlic, minced
¼ teaspoon marjoram
¼ teaspoon thyme

1. If you are using fresh green beans, snap and steam for approximately 5 minutes, until tender but not soft. For frozen, cook according to package directions, until firm and bright green. Drain and set aside.
2. Melt butter in large skillet. Add mushrooms, onions, and garlic and sauté until onions and mushrooms are soft. Stir in marjoram and thyme.
3. Just before serving add beans to skillet, toss in melted butter mixture, cover, and allow to heat through, about 5 minutes.

Easy Onion Rolls

2 cups flour
½ teaspoon salt
1 tablespoon baking powder
½ cup butter or butter-flavored vegetable
   shortening
½ cup sour cream

½ cup milk
2 tablespoons butter
1 small red onion
1 small white onion
½ teaspoon ground thyme
1 teaspoon rosemary leaves

1. Preheat oven to 425 degrees. Lightly grease or spray cookie sheet.
2. In a large mixing bowl, blend dry ingredients. Cut in butter until mixture resembles coarse meal. Add sour cream and stir until barely mixed.
3. Add milk and mix or knead until a rich elastic dough forms. Set aside.
4. In a heavy skillet over medium heat, melt 2 tablespoons butter and sauté chopped onions with spices until soft and transparent. Cool slightly.
5. Roll out dough in a large rectangle approximately ¼ inch thick.
6. Spread onion mixture over dough, and roll into a tight log.
7. Cut into 1-inch slices and place approximately ½ inch apart on cookie sheet. Bake for 15 minutes.

VARIATION: For a sweet breakfast treat, omit the onion mixture. Add 2 teaspoons of dried orange peel and ½ cup sugar to the dough (mix in with the flour). Spread rolled dough with 4 to 6 tablespoons of butter, and sprinkle with a mixture of ½ cup brown sugar, ¼ cup white sugar, and 2 tablespoons cinnamon. Top with 1 cup chopped nuts and ½ cup raisins if desired. Prepare and bake as directed above. While still quite warm from the oven, frost with a glaze of 1 cup powdered sugar thinned with 2 tablespoons orange juice or warm water.

Buttermilk Pound Cake

Makes 2 pound cakes (they store well in the freezer)

4 sticks butter, softened
3⅓ cups sugar
6 eggs, beaten
1 tablespoon vanilla extract
3½ cups flour

1 teaspoon baking soda
2 teaspoons baking powder
1 teaspoon salt
1 teaspoon mace
2 cups buttermilk

1. Preheat oven to 350 degrees. Spray or butter and flour baking pans.
2. Cream butter and sugar until thick. Add eggs and vanilla extract and beat well.
3. In a separate bowl, combine flour, soda, powder, salt, and mace. Add to egg mixture alternately with the buttermilk, beating well after each addition.
4. Pour batter into 2 large, greased loaf pans and bake 45 to 50 minutes, or 1 bundt cake pan and bake 1 hour and 15 minutes, until a knife inserted in center comes out clean. Cool. Serve slices topped with Coconut Dessert Salsa.

Coconut Dessert Salsa

4 tablespoons peanut oil
½ cup brown sugar
¼ teaspoon allspice
½ teaspoon lemon peel
4 tablespoons Curaçao or other orange-flavored liqueur

1 cup chopped pecans
1 20-ounce can pineapple chunks, drained
1 11-ounce can mandarin oranges, drained
⅔ cup shredded, sweetened coconut

1. Combine oil, brown sugar, allspice, lemon peel, and liquor in medium sauce pan over medium-high heat and stir until well mixed.
2. Add pecans and toss until well coated with sugar syrup.
3. Remove from heat and gently toss pineapple and oranges in the syrup.
4. Fold in coconut. Serve at room temperature or refrigerate until ready to use.

The Double Heart Brand
a working-day meal for 6 to 8 hungry hands

*Saying "I love you" is the easiest way
to start something big or end something small.*

Riatas swing loosely and glide through air thick with smoke from the branding fire. One after another, bawling calves are caught and quickly marked with the outfit's return address. A group of his friends are throwing catch ropes. There is no cash pay for these extra cowhands, just the promise of help in turn and a hearty meal. As the ranch manager's new wife, that job falls to you.

Branding is a celebration, a gathering not only of cattle but of neighbors and friends and of a way of life in tune with the land, strong enough to survive years on the plains, yet still easily rustled by mother nature's whims. When you're part of the crew, there is little time to fuss over delicate dinners.

A cut little-used outside of cow camps and barbecue joints, BRISKET makes an easy indoor barbecue. Liquid smoke is a true culinary mystery. Tucked away among the condiments at your local grocery, it tastes like a campfire in a tidy little bottle.

Don't be scared off by the hours for OVERNIGHT BEANS. These frijoles simply happen—with little attention and even less effort. While out with the wagon, cowboys often kept the same pot bubbling for several days. You can't cook beans too long.

It is the sauce that makes any barbecue special. Make this DEEP-RED POURING SAUCE a day or two in advance; it ladles welcome western flavor over everything from rice to cheese-topped baked potatoes.

After warm rolls, CREAMY COLESLAW, and soothing CORN BREAD PUDDING, your spread will have eager help next time branding rolls around.

Oven Barbecue Brisket

Tin foil
3 teaspoons salt
1½ teaspoons black pepper
1½ teaspoons garlic
¾ teaspoon chili powder
   (or more to suit your taste)

½ teaspoon cayenne pepper
   (or more or less to suit your taste)
3-pound brisket (approximately)
6 tablespoons liquid smoke
3 tablespoons worcestershire sauce
1 jalapeño, cut in half

1. Preheat oven to 250 degrees.
2. Mix dry ingredients and rub into both sides of the meat.
3. With brisket resting on 2 layers of tin foil, mix liquid smoke and worcestershire sauce and pour over both sides of meat.
4. Top meat with jalapeño and seal tightly inside foil, so liquid can't leak out.
5. Bake for 5½ to 6 hours on center rack. Check the meat after about 4 hours to make sure it isn't drying out. If necessary, add a bit of water or more liquid smoke to the tin-foil packet. Close securely before returning to oven.

Deep-Red Pouring Sauce

1 large onion, chopped
¼ cup olive oil
1 teaspoon salt
1½ teaspoons black pepper
2 teaspoons garlic powder
1–2½ teaspoons chili powder (to taste)
12-ounce jar chili sauce
29-ounce can tomato sauce
½ cup honey
½ cup molasses
½ cup brown sugar

¼–1 teaspoon red pepper flakes (to taste)
1 teaspoon paprika
1 teaspoon dried orange peel
*1–3 jalapeños (fresh or canned), seeded
    and chopped (depending on your taste)*
2 tablespoons dry mustard
1 teaspoon cinnamon
2 tablespoons lemon juice
2 tablespoons ketchup
3 tablespoons worcestershire sauce

1. In a large saucepan, sauté onions in olive oil until translucent.
2. Add salt, pepper, garlic powder and chili powder and allow to cook two minutes more, stirring often.
3. Add remaining ingredients and cook over medium heat (sauce should be bubbling) for 1½ to 2 hours, until sauce is thick and flavors are well blended.

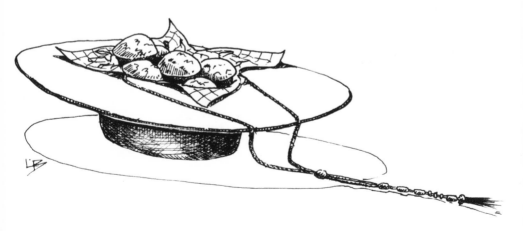

Creamy Coleslaw

For the Salad

½ small head of green cabbage, shredded
  or chopped
½ small head of purple cabbage, shredded
  or chopped
1 red onion, chopped
3 carrots, peeled and chopped

For the Dressing

¾ cup mayonnaise
¾ cup buttermilk
1½ tablespoons sugar
2 teaspoons celery seeds
1 teaspoon salt
¼ teaspoon black pepper
2 tablespoons prepared mustard
1½ tablespoons cider vinegar
¼ cup salted peanuts

1. Toss chopped cabbage, onions, and carrots together in large bowl.
2. In a separate bowl, mix together all dressing ingredients.
3. Pour dressing over cabbage mixture; toss well to coat.
4. Sprinkle with salted peanuts.
5. Chill at least ½ hour before serving.

Overnight Baked Beans

1 pound pinto beans
1 whole onion
3 bay leaves
5 strips bacon
½ cup molasses
½ cup honey
½ cup brown sugar
1 28-ounce can crushed tomatoes

½ cup orange juice
1 cup raisins
1 teaspoon chili powder
½ teaspoon cayenne pepper
1 jalapeño, fresh or canned
Salt and pepper to taste
¼ cup cider vinegar

1. In the morning, cover beans with water in a large cooking pot and allow to soak all day.
2. At night, add enough warm water to cover the beans by three inches, whole onion, bay leaves, and bacon.
3. Cover pot and place in a 250-degree oven and cook overnight (about 8 to 10 hours).
4. In the morning, drain out some of cooking water so beans are just barely covered. Add all the remaining ingredients and return to oven for 4 hours.
5. Uncover beans and cook 2½ hours longer.

Note: Remember to check every so often so the beans don't dry out. If they need it, add a bit of warm water now and again, and leave the pot uncovered for the last 2½ hours for a hearty pot with thick, flavorful sauce.

Corn Bread Pudding

½ of a 7 x 11 pan of corn bread
   (See Sweet Breakfast Corn Bread on
   page 16), sliced approximately
   ½-inch thick
6 tablespoons butter
1 apple, peeled, cored, quartered, and
   sliced in ¼-inch slices

1 cup golden raisins
4 eggs
½ cup brown sugar
¼ cup white sugar
4 cups milk
2 tablespoons vanilla extract
¼ teaspoon nutmeg

1. Preheat oven to 300 degrees.
2. Butter corn bread slices and arrange in single layers (butter-sides down) in Dutch oven, ovenproof bowl, or baking dish. Add a sprinkling of apple slices and raisins. Repeat with remaining bread, apples, and raisins.
3. Cream eggs and sugar. Add milk and vanilla and mix until well blended.
4. Pour milk mixture over bread layers and allow to sit for 30 minutes.
5. Sprinkle top with nutmeg, then bake for 1½ hours, or until knife inserted in center comes out clean. Serve with Lemon Hard Sauce.

Lemon Hard Sauce

1 stick butter, softened
1⅓ cups confectioners sugar
2 teaspoons brandy or brandy extract

¼ teaspoon lemon peel
1 tablespoon lemon juice
2 tablespoons warm water

1. Cream butter and sugar until thick and lemon colored.
2. Add remaining ingredients and stir with wooden spoon until smooth and well blended.
3. Serve spooned over the piping-hot pudding.

Won't You Be Mine?
a romantic dinner for 4 to 6

"It's the face powder that get's a man interested,
but it's the baking powder that keeps him home." —Gene Hackman
as Buck Barrow in Arthur Penn's big-screen classic, Bonnie and Clyde

Holding your hand across the table, he gently calls you "Querida…Darling." Not just another dinner together, tonight is an event, a treasured memory you'll hold in your heart.

Glide deliciously into the evening with SWEET POTATO SOUP, sweetened by rich honey and sparked by zesty cayenne pepper. With brandy and fresh cream, the delicate orange bisque is an easy starter that feels like an occasion.

Mellowed by slow cooking, the TRIPLE-ONION FLANK STEAK's filling is softly bittersweet, tuned by herbs and deep red wine.

BUTTERMILK BISCUITS are a culinary tradition of the western lands, served for every meal. Cowboys brag about the "pot wrassler" who makes the lightest biscuits, while home cooks take pride in kneading together hot, flaky breads. Topped with cream gravy or lightly capped with sweet butter and honey, these western specialties are traditionally cut round with baking powder tins. Or, use your favorite cookie cutter—a heart, diamond, or cheery flower—for powdery breads that celebrate the occasion.

For dessert, create a thick velvet custard. Slow cooked and pampered on the stove, a bit of steady patience magically turns eggs, milk, and sugar into a heavenly cloud, wrapped in a slightly chocolate shell. This certainly is not the kind of dish wagon cooks served to hungry cowboys. It's a special, carefully created merit badge of romance.

In candlelit corners tucked away in quiet restaurants or cozy warm kitchens, our best moments seem to happen in the delightful company of good food and good friends.

Sweet Potato Soup

3 large sweet potatoes, peeled and cut into
 1-inch cubes
2 carrots, peeled and cut into 1-inch slices
1 sweet red pepper, cored, seeded, and
 chopped (reserve some for garnish)
½ medium onion, coarsely chopped
3 14½-ounce cans chicken broth, or
 6 cups homemade

6 tablespoons honey
4 tablespoons butter
2 teaspoons salt
¼ teaspoon cayenne pepper
¼ cup brandy
¾ cup cream

1. Combine all the chopped vegetables in a stockpot and cover with chicken stock. Bring to a slow boil and cook partially covered 45 minutes to 1 hour, until potatoes begin to break apart.
2. In the blender, purée vegetables and stock in small batches and set aside.
3. Heat honey and butter in stockpot, stirring constantly until butter melts. Add puréed vegetables, 2 cups at a time, stirring until well blended before adding more.
4. After adding all the purée, add spices, brandy, and cream, and allow to simmer (not boil) 25 minutes, until flavors are blended and soup is warm throughout.
5. Garnish with chopped red bell peppers.

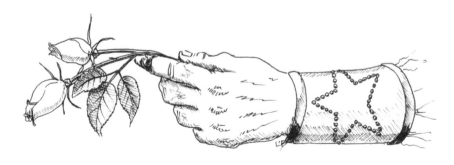

Triple-Onion Flank Steak

1 approximately 2-pound flank steak

For the Marinade
½ cup red wine
½ cup olive oil
2 tablespoons lemon juice
1 teaspoon rosemary
½ teaspoon garlic powder
¼ teaspoon salt

For the Stuffing
1 10-ounce carton pearl onions
3 tablespoons butter
3 green onions, chopped
½ red onion, chopped
⅛ teaspoon salt
¼ teaspoon pepper
⅛ teaspoon thyme

1. Tenderize flank steak with kitchen mallet.
2. Combine marinade ingredients in locking plastic bag or oblong baking pan, add meat, and refrigerate for 1 hour.
3. Preheat oven to 350 degrees.
4. Boil pearl onions in water for three minutes, drain, and cut off one end so the skins will easily slide off. Let cool, then cut in half.
5. Melt butter in a small saucepan, add pearl onions and remaining ingredients for the stuffing, and sauté until translucent.
6. Remove steak from marinade, lay flat on work surface, and spread top with the slightly cooled onion mixture.
7. Tightly roll the steak in jelly-roll fashion and secure with toothpicks or tie with kitchen twine at 2-inch intervals.
8. Bake for 1 hour and 45 minutes to 2 hours, until cooked through and tender, basting occasionally with the pan juices.

Note: For a delicious and easy gravy, heat pan drippings with 1½ cups sour cream, stirring constantly until just heated through.

Buttermilk Biscuits

Makes about 12 fluffy biscuits

2 cups flour
2 teaspoons baking powder
1 teaspoon baking soda

½ teaspoon salt
⅓ cup vegetable shortening
¾ cup buttermilk

1. Preheat oven to 425 degrees.
2. Mix flour, powder, soda, and salt in a large mixing bowl.
3. Cut in shortening until mixture resembles coarse meal.
4. Add buttermilk and stir until just blended.
5. Turn out dough onto a lightly floured work surface and knead a few times until dough is smooth and elastic. Do not over-knead. Roll dough to ½ inch thick, cut with biscuit cutter or baking-powder can.
7. Place on baking sheet so they are just touching, and bake for 10 to 12 minutes.

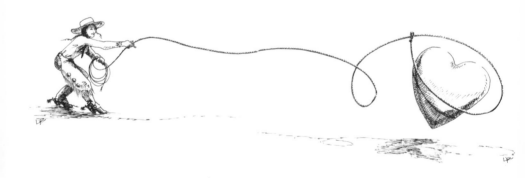

Layered Rice

3 tablespoons butter
3 tablespoons flour
2 cups milk
¼ teaspoon garlic powder
¼ teaspoon salt
⅛ teaspoon black pepper
1½ teaspoons parsley flakes

1 large tomato, cut into thin slices
2 cups cooked rice
1 cup frozen peas, defrosted
¾ cup shredded flavorful cheese (Swiss or
   Parmesan is nice)
2 tablespoons seasoned bread crumbs

1. Preheat oven to 350 degrees. Spray or butter casserole.
2. In a small saucepan, melt butter. Stir in flour and cook over medium heat, stirring constantly, until a thick paste forms.
3. Continue stirring while slowly adding milk to thin the mixture. When all the milk is added, cook 3 to 5 minutes, stirring occasionally, until thick.
4. Remove from heat and blend in garlic powder, salt, pepper, and parsley flakes. Set aside.
5. Line the bottom of a well-buttered casserole dish with a single layer of tomato slices. Top with half the rice.
6. Sprinkle with peas. Cover with remaining rice, and another single layer of tomato slices. With a knife, make several cuts straight through the layers of rice and vegetable so the cream sauce will run throughout the dish.
7. Pour cream sauce over entire layered casserole.
8. Sprinkle top with shredded cheese, cover lightly with bread crumbs, and bake 35 minutes, until cheese is melted and mixture is bubbly.

Velvet Custard

6 egg yolks
1½ tablespoons cornstarch
⅓ cup sugar

2 cups milk
1 teaspoon vanilla

1. In a medium saucepan or the top of a double boiler, whisk together the egg yolk, cornstarch, and sugar over medium-low heat.
2. Add the milk in a thin stream, stirring constantly.
3. Cook over medium heat until a thick custard forms. This could take up to an hour. Stir often and relax, the custard will thicken.
4. Remove from heat and stir in the vanilla. Transfer to a kitchen bowl and cool completely.
5. Serve in Cocoa Meringue Kisses.

Note: To speed the custard cooling, rest the bowl in cold water.

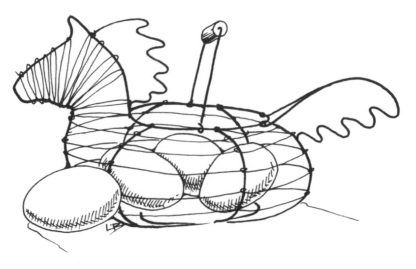

Cocoa Meringue Kisses

6 egg whites, room temperature
¼ teaspoon salt
½ teaspoon cream of tartar
1½ teaspoons vanilla

2 cups sugar
¾ cup cocoa
1 cup chopped pecans
Baking parchment or waxed paper

1. Preheat oven to 250 degrees.
2. In a large mixing bowl, combine egg whites, salt, cream of tartar, and vanilla.
3. Beat with a mixer on high speed until soft peaks form.
4. While beating, gradually add sugar and whip until mixture is shiny and mounds in firm peaks.
5. Fold in cocoa and nuts by hand or with mixer on lowest speed.
6. For cookies, drop by large spoonfuls (about 1½ to 2 inches across) onto cookie sheet lined with baking parchment paper. With your fingers, pinch tops to form peaks resembling "kiss" shapes.
7. For custard shells, drop by ½ cupfuls onto prepared baking sheets, leaving ½ to 2 inches between meringues. Using the back of a spoon, shape a cavity in each meringue round to hold the filling.
8. Bake 45 to 60 minutes, until kisses are dry but not browned. To crisp meringues, you may need to turn off the oven, holding the door open with a kitchen spoon, for another 10 to 15 minutes.
9. Remove from paper while still warm.
10. When cool, just before serving, fill with chilled custard and dust top with a sprinkling of cocoa powder and a dollop of whipped cream if desired.

Note: In dry climates, store meringues in an airtight container. In damp or humid areas, freeze to retain freshness.

Index

The Author and Artists

KATHY LYNN WILLS is a freelance writer specializing in cowboy culture and cooking. She is a regular contributor to both *Cowboy* and *Cowboys and Indians* magazines. In addition, she is the proprietor of the Cowboy Country General Store, a catalog.

LINDA BARK'KARIE (illustrations throughout the recipes) is a western artist who specializes in black and white, primarily graphite. Her unique artistic approach has received numerous awards and her fine art prints can be found in galleries and private collections throughout the United States and Europe.

LINDA K. GAGE (illustrations on cover and chapter openings) is an illustrator and fine artist who works in pen and ink, pencil, watercolor, and pastel. She specializes in portraiture, children, landscapes, and western art. Her fine art prints can be found in galleries and western gift shops.

JOELLE SMITH (author's portrait) is a western artist who works exclusively in watercolor. Her prints and originals are available at western art galleries and through Rosenbo Paint Company.